MW01252661

"The Voice of the Assistant P
ing and often thankless position of assistant principal
through her well thought out questions, narrative, and conversations with several practitioners the balancing act that each assistant principal must manage between the often competing priorities of instructional leadership, school culture, and student discipline.

This book is a valuable resource for any classroom educator contemplating a move into building leadership and provides a clear glimpse into current issues faced by nearly every assistant principal.

The book also dispels the stereotype of the assistant principal portrayed in movies and popular cultural and presents compelling portraits of caring educators who want the best for the students they serve.

These stories show the complexity of the role of assistant principal and the nuances and high level of skills required to do the job effectively."

– Kevin McIntyre, Ed.D.
Superintendent, Milford Public Schools

— oOo —

"**Next In Line to Lead: The Voice of the Assistant Principal** (Vol.1) text is sure to do two very important things in the context of education- Inform and Inspire! Current and aspiring assistant principals can expect to learn from the voices of professionals with experiences ranging from 2 to 11 years on topics focused on important characteristics of effective and exemplary leadership and probably most importantly recommendations and strategies for becoming a principal.

The Creator, Sharon H. Porter, Ed.D., has more than 25 years of experience in education and shaped her professional journey by assisting first and second-year assistant principals reach their optimal capacity in their roles. Porter has eloquently used her own experiences as an administrator as a conceptual framework to advance the efforts of professionals in the field of education."

– Joelle Davis Carter, Ph.D.
Dean for Student Development, Piedmont Community College

— oOo —

"**Next in Line to Lead** is an interesting anthology of both personal and professional journeys from the viewpoint of the assistant principal. The book offers valuable insights from the assistant principal perspective including recommendations on how to increase leadership capacity, build a positive school climate and personal reflections on what inspired them to take on the challenge of school leadership.

Reading their stories is sure to give the novice school leader a dose of encouragement while giving the seasoned school leader a reminder of the importance and unique challenges of the assistant principal role. Sharon Porter has provided those of us interested in leadership development a new tool with which to launch powerful discussions regarding the principal pipeline."

– Paula Huffman, Director of Talent Development
Department of Human Resources and Talent Development
Loudoun County Public Schools

— oOo —

"Taking the reader on the professional journey of nine aspiring school leaders, Dr. Porter's innovative and inspiring anthology provides a road map for district leaders and Principals on their role in developing and nurturing the next generation of successful school leaders.

Dr. Porter and her subjects reflect on what it takes to be an effective leader in today's public schools and the proactive engagement necessary of the assistant principal to prepare for the day they are selected as the next in line to lead. This is a must read for any aspiring school leader as well as district staff who are charged with ensuring that a strong pipeline of leaders are ready to take on the challenging role of the Principal."

– Crystal Scillitani
Leadership Coach and Former Principal,
Leading Up Consulting

NEXT IN LINE TO LEAD

The Voice of the Assistant Principal

Volume I

(First Edition)

Sharon Hargro Porter, Ed.D.

Foreword by Barry Z. Posner, Ph.D.

ISBN-13: 978-0692884348
ISBN-10: 0692884343

Printed in the United States of America

Dedication

Next In Line to Lead: The Voice of the Assistant Principal Volume 1 First Edition is dedicated to the amazing assistant principals that I was fortunate to have during my tenure as principal in Maryland and North Carolina.

Anne-Marie, Raquel, James, Toni, and Kimberly; you were all exceptional instructional leaders, self-starters, and you took ownership in your development as a leader. But, most importantly, your loyalty was undeniable. You pushed back when appropriate, you established your "leader voice", and you were indeed the assistant PRINCIPAL and not the principal's ASSISTANT!

Table of Contents

Foreword

It's really all about the kids! Every teacher and every teacher turned school administrator, as attested to by the cases in this volume, did so because of how they were treated when they were students in their schools. And the most effective principals, of any rank, never forget that the bottom line in any decision about curriculum, bus schedules, salaries, cafeteria menus, cultural and athletic activities, campus hours, and the like is "what's in the best interests of the kids going to this school?"

Going back to basics, the culture foundation and effectiveness of every school depends upon "tone at the top" — the leadership at that institution. Scores of studies have documented that schools recognized for sustained academic achievements have principals that understand the importance of leadership, and engage more frequently in The Five Practices of Exemplary Leadership© than their counterparts: schools with less of a learning environment. The students, teachers, and staff in every school warrant good leadership, and the best leaders, like those chronicled in this volume, strongly believe that the people at their schools deserve the very best leadership that they can provide.

Similarly, the importance of mentors, coaches, and role models is underscored by all of the stories these assistant principals tell. You can't become the best leader you can be all by yourself. Indeed, a key element in overcoming any adversity is having a stable supportive relationship with another person, and each of the case studies documents how the support and encouragement of a teacher or school administrator made a tremendous difference in their lives and careers. You should read this book with this perspective in mind; both for you and in thinking about the difference you are making in the lives of those around you. Our own research has found that people who have high-quality connections are healthier, have higher cognitive functioning, are broader thinkers, are more resilient, are more committed to the organization, and have better judgement when trusting others.

Educational institutions face great challenges and thus need great leaders. It comes as no surprise, that *Challenge the Process* was mentioned most often as the leadership practice those "next-in-line-to-lead" embraced in their leadership journeys. Living in a cave doesn't make you a geologist, nor do years of experience alone make you an expert. These cases clearly demonstrate the importance of continually putting yourself in positions where you can learn (that is, experiment, make mistakes, and try again). You'll find this book helpful if you can savor their experiences; realizing that seldom does anyone get it right the first time and that no one is ever smarter than everyone else.

Leadership makes a difference. Think about the *worst* and *best* principals you've ever worked with. I recently asked a group of teachers studying for their school administrative credential to estimate the percent of their talents (time, energy, commitment) that their *worst* principal brought forth from them. The average was a little bit more than 30 percent. The average when they thought about their *best* principal was over 95 percent. That's a three-fold increase in productivity: same people, different leaders. What sort of difference do you want to make?

Barry Z. Posner, PhD
Accolti Professor of Leadership
Santa Clara University
Co-author: The Leadership Challenge and Learning Leadership

Preface

Leadership Development is one of my educational passions. I was inspired to create **Next In Line to Lead** when conducting my literature review for my dissertation on principal preparation. My professional career, my dissertation, as well as this project's focus, is to prepare a bench of leaders for the principalship. The Principal Pipeline is designed to recruit, hire, induct, prepare and develop effective leaders. Succession planning should be a part of every school district's overall strategic plan and should be a deliberate focus for district administrators.

The Wallace Report *"The Making of the Principal: Five Lessons in Leadership Training"*, contends that principals need high-quality mentoring and professional development tailored to the individual and district needs. It is my belief that the developmental needs of the assistant principal are similar, if not the same, if we are to effectively prepare them to be next in line to lead. Principal preparation has been a focus in recent years. School districts have adopted or revised their leader standards, partnered with universities to create programs that align with district initiatives, assigned mentors and/

or coaches to aspiring and new administrators, all as a concerted effort to prepare "The Next In Line to Lead".

I currently serve as a Leadership Development Coach in a large urban school district in the Washington, D.C. Metropolitan area. My responsibilities in this role include coaching first and second year principals and assistant principals. I also serve as the coordinator for the induction program for first and second year assistant principals in my school district. The passion to serve and develop leaders led me to explore a more global view on the preparation of school leaders.

Assistant principals come into the position with varied experiences. Many enter administration directly from the classroom, while others may have experience as teacher leaders and have held positions out of the classroom prior to being appointed as assistant principal. The size of the school district also may play a critical role in the development of assistant principals. In speaking with school leaders in rural school districts, I have learned that oftentimes, there is no designated department, office or program that specifically provides development for aspiring principals. Many smaller school districts are not even structured to have assistant principals.

Principals most commonly are chosen from the pool of assistant principals. Research has indicated that the assistant principal position does not provide appropriate training or preparation for assistant principals to become principals. My question is why not? Given the impact school leadership can have on student outcomes, providing every school with an effective principal should clearly be among the top priorities. The goal of providing every school with an effective principal should definitely include an intentional focus on preparing assistant principals to lead schools while in their current role.

Acknowledgements

First, I would like to acknowledge **Taurea Avant** for her work with authors across the United States and very soon other countries. She is the reason I started publishing my writing. She has inspired, encouraged, and most importantly, taught me the value of authorship.

I would also like to acknowledge **Devay Campbell**. A thought and accountability partner like no other; Devay helped cultivate my idea of putting this project together. She is gifted with providing clarity and is the "Queen of follow-up"!

Finally, I would like to acknowledge my Foreword Author, **Dr. Barry Z. Posner.** His book *The Leadership Challenge* was instrumental in my development as an assistant principal looking to make the leap into the principalship.

Introduction

"Leadership is second only to classroom instruction among all school-related factors that contribute to what students learn at school." (Leithwood, Louise, Anderson, & Wahlstrom, 2004)

Next In Line to Lead: The Voice of the Assistant Principal Volume 1 features assistant principals from California, Georgia, Maryland, New Jersey, South Carolina, and Texas. They have a total of 50 years of experience as assistant principals, ranging from two to eleven years. They represent Elementary, Middle, and High school levels.

The position of assistant principal was originally introduced into schools in the United States in the 1930s designed primarily as a support to reduce principal workload (Harvey, 1994) – (Principal's Assistant). With increased accountability for student achievement, the primary role of assistant principal has evolved from that of disciplinarian and school operations manager to instructional leader (Assistant Principal). Although assistant principals continue to have responsibilities with school discipline, bus and lunch schedules; a focus on instruction is now part of an assistant principal's workday. In order for assistant principals to be effective instructional leaders: the support of the building principal is needed. Intentional professional development with a focus on principal preparation is needed as well as opportunities for assistant principals to engage in authentic activities that require instructional leadership.

Duties and responsibilities of an assistant principal may vary from school district to school district and school to school. When I meet assistant principals either in a professional setting or a social setting, I always ask two questions: Do you have aspirations to pursue the principalship? Does your work as an assistant principal allow you to feel a level of readiness to assume the role of principal?

In *Next in Line to Lead: The Voice of the Assistant Principal* First Edition, each of the nine assistant principals responded to the following questions:

- What motivated or inspired you to become an assistant principal?
- Bambrick-Santoyo (2012) in *Leverage Leadership* identifies seven core areas of school leadership, which are referred to as levers. What experiences have you had as an assistant principal in each of the seven core areas identified?

  Instructional Levers:
  1. Data-driven instruction
  2. Observation and feedback
  3. Instructional planning
  4. Professional development

  Cultural Levers:
  1. Student culture
  2. Staff culture
  3. Managing school leadership teams

- What specific experiences in your tenure as an assistant principal have allowed you to increase your readiness to assume the role of principal?
- In the book *The Leadership Challenge* Kouzes and Posner (2002) identify "Five Practices of Exemplary Leadership". Choose one of the five practices and explain how you currently demonstrate that practice.

  Model the Way
  Inspire a Shared Vision
  Challenge the Process
  Enable Others to Act
  Encourage the Heart

- What activities and learning experiences do you recommend for assistant principals aspiring to assume the role of principal?

- What do you believe are five (5) key characteristics of effective leader-ship? Describe how you demonstrate each of those characteristics.
- In the book, *School Culture Rewired*, Steve Gruenert and Todd Whitaker (2015) explains the difference in school climate and school culture as the climate represents the weather today and school culture represents the weather over a long period of time.
- When you are appointed principal, how would you assess the current status of your new school's climate and culture? Identify the characteristics of a school with a positive climate and culture.

Each year, school districts are recruiting, interviewing, selecting, and hiring to fill vacancies left by principals who retire, are promoted, or leave the profession altogether. Who will fill those vacancies? In the voice of the assistant principal, these nine educational leaders are confidently claiming they are **NEXT IN LINE TO LEAD**!

Sharon H. Porter
Creator, Next In Line to Lead Book Series

Sandra Bobo

"It is important for leaders to have a passion for the work that they do." – S. Bobo

What motivated or inspired you to become an Assistant Principal?

Upon graduating from college, I came back home to the Washington, D.C. area looking for work within my field. I landed a job working as a Training Specialist in one of the four largest limousine companies in the world. As an English major, I was required to create and design training manuals for individuals that were new and within the company that worked in the reservations and dispatch departments. As a young college graduate, I was impressed that I was able to travel all across the U.S. to train employees in the field, as well as attend three Super Bowls, BET Awards, Grammys, etc. After all of that, I was still unhappy. Within my sorority, I had always worked in the community to give back. One particular afternoon, I worked with young ladies that were placed in a youth detention center. After receiving an epiphany, I knew it was time for me to leave Corporate America and work with the youth. I began teaching English to students in grades nine and ten. A wonderful assistant principal (AP) who automatically took me under her wings mentored me.

Originally, I thought about becoming a Professional School Counselor, but my AP Mentor and former Principal said my demeanor would be more suitable to go into administration. I later went back to school to obtain my Masters in Educational Administration. My AP Mentor affectionately made me the 2004 class sponsor so that we were able to work well together and maintain our close relationship. We were such a match made in heaven! Then came graduation day – June 10, 2004. Our students were so excited to walk across the stage with the guidance of my AP Mentor and myself. My AP Mentor never made it to graduation and we later received word that day she was involved in a car accident and later died...on graduation day. Needless to say, I lost a best friend, sister and mentor; but I was determined to carry on her legacy and be the best Assistant Principal ever.

Bambrick-Santoyo (2012) identifies seven core areas of school leadership, which are referred to as levers in the book *Leverage Leadership:* What experiences have you had as an assistant principal in each of the seven core areas identified?

Instructional Levers:

1. *Data-driven instruction* – I had the privilege and opportunity to attend DataWise training at Harvard University. I used to be so fearful of hearing the word "DATA", but now I can say that I feel a little more comfortable when hearing and using the word. Our county focuses on data whether it is with attendance, suspension, and/or testing.

2. *Observation and feedback* – I oversee the English department. I conduct formal and informal observations and provide feedback to teachers. I also spearhead the Learning Walks that occur in our building with members of the School Based Leadership Team (SBLT). It's good for the members of the SBLT to see how effective their colleagues are teaching within the classroom.

3. *Instructional planning* – I attend weekly collaborative planning with members of the English department. We use data from previous assessments to align our lesson plans accordingly.

4. *Professional development* – As the administrator who also oversees Special Education, I try to find professional development to suit the needs of the teachers that are seeking additional support to maintain their IEPs. It's important for teachers as well as administrators to partake in PDs that will enhance, develop, and make them grow both personally and professionally.

Cultural Levers:

1. *Student culture* – With a school of 740 students (grades 9 – 12) the culture and climate has already been established from the former principal that was here previously for seven years. It felt good to enter a building where the student culture is strong. The students are familiar with the proficiency of the school and its norms. With the increase of the graduation rate from the previous year, the outgoing seniors are "in tuned" and are encouraging each other to surmount pass the previous graduating class and aim higher.

2. *Staff culture* – Our staff is familiar with the mission statement of the school: Provide, Promote, Prepare. The majority of the staff wants to do what's best for students. Staff culture permeates from the top down. As educators, it's important to perform and demonstrate a positive culture, as our students know if or when tension is brewing. Being highly visible for students and staff can produce big results.

3. *Managing school leadership teams* – "Everyone wants to become an administrator but no one wants to put in the work." I hear this quote all the time from many of my colleagues. Leaders lead people while managers manage tasks. Finding and identifying instructional leaders is the key. Within our building, we have a dynamic Leadership Council team which meets every first Tuesday of the month. Within this group, the

leadership council team serves as instructional supervisors and is the voice of the administration. They also effectively plan, lead data, and provide feedback to others.

In the book *Leadership Challenge,* Kouzes and Posner (2002) identify "Five Practices of Exemplary Leadership". Choose one of the five practices and explain how you currently demonstrate that practice.

Encourage the Heart – It is so important to build and maintain staff culture with the employees. I personally demonstrate this particular practice ALL of the time. I always show appreciation for the contribution of teachers/staff (as well as students) whether it is with a mere thank you, a smile, a note, or even an email.

What activities and learning experiences do you recommend for assistant principals aspiring to assume the role of principal?

- Shadow principals outside of your building.
- Seek and attend any professional development that may be offered.
- Stay up-to-date with the latest articles.
- Ask questions and seek proper guidance.

What do you believe are five (5) key characteristics of effective leadership? Describe how you demonstrate each of those characteristics.

Passion – It is important for leaders to have a passion for the work that they do. I always motivate the staff and encourage them to become more productive.

Communication – Communicating and sharing your vision is vital. Allowing and opening the doors of communication is essential to developing and establishing a bond with others. No one should feel uncomfortable to come to you and speak about anything.

Detail Orientated – Most of my colleagues make fun of me because I have a tendency to be "overly" detail orientated. It's good to always plan ahead and set the right people in place in order to execute the plans.

Honesty – Obstacles can be addressed rather than avoided when honesty is involved. It is important for an effective leader to maintain honesty.

Consistency – To maintain and gain buy-in from staff, a leader should be consistent. By showing and being an example of fairness and obtaining credibility, your staff will more than likely will act the same way.

In the book *School Culture Rewired,* Steve Gruenert and Todd Whitaker (2015) explains the difference in school climate and school culture as the climate represents the weather today and school culture represents the weather over a long period of time (overall).

When you are appointed principal, how would you assess the current status of your new school's climate and culture? Identify the characteristics of a school with a positive climate and culture.

When I am appointed principal, I would sit and meet with each and every staff member individually to see and hear his or her expectations of me. I would then plan to meet with parents as well as students for a "meet and greet". Depending on the circumstances of the previous principal would determine whether or not I would be able to seek guidance from him or her. It takes time to seek and learn the budget, facilities, discipline, school safety, student assessment, and teacher evaluation. Maintaining a positive culture and climate will always determine the outcome.

What educational leaders are saying about Sandra Bobo:

"What makes Ms. Bobo an effective leader is her uncanny ability to remain positive and focused in the areas of student achievement and building teacher capacity. She embodies positivity and works at building and supporting a positive school culture. She tackles tough conversations with students, staff and parents alike which cause reflection and growth. She is a team player and demonstrates a readiness to help all who ask."

– Katrina Lamont, Current Supervisor

"She is excellent with engaging parents, community and stakeholders in the educational process; she creates and maintains a positive school culture for staff and students; she is creative and uses technology to support instruction, communicate with parents and market the school."

– Kristi Holden, Ed.D., Former Supervisor

Ms. Sandra Bobo is currently a High School Assistant Principal located in Maryland. She received a Bachelor of Arts degree in English with a minor in Mass Communications from Virginia State University and earned a Master of Science degree from Trinity College in Educational Administration.

Ms. Bobo started her career as a High School English teacher in 2001 and was appointed an assistant principal in 2008.

Ms. Bobo has earned certificates from Emerging Leaders – New Leaders, Maryland State Department of Education (MSDE), Aspiring Principals Institute, Harvard University – Instructional Rounds, and was a member of the first cohort of the Assistant Principal Induction Program (APIP) in her school district.

Ms. Bobo is a proud mother of two teenage daughters and is an active member of several organizations such as the Association of Supervision & Curriculum Development (ASCD), American Society of Training & Development, Phi Delta Kappa International, National Alliance of Black School Educators (NABSE), National Association of Secondary School Principals (NASSP), National Educators Association (NEA) and Delta Sigma Theta Sorority, Inc.

Ms. Bobo believes that it is important to have very high expectations set for each and every student and have the adults held accountable for their actions.

"It is best to lead by example than by decree." – Author Unknown

Darren A. Clay

"Effective leadership in the K-12 sector requires school leaders to demonstrate 'Grit.'" – D. Clay

What motivated or inspired you to become an assistant principal?

My motivation to become a school leader stems from a genealogy of school and district leaders. My family's school leadership lineage dates to 1930 as my great-grandfather served as a school headmaster for over 15 years. In addition, both my mother and father served as school principals in South Florida. A more direct correlation for my ascension into school leadership stems from my father's position as an Assistant Principal at the middle school that I attended as a youth along with my mother's recognition as District Teacher of the Year Runner-Up in the 5th largest school district in the country. I believe it's safe to say that "I followed in my parents' footsteps". After earning Teacher of the Year honors in just my second year of teaching, my desire to lead teachers increased exponentially. As I began to take the lead on various committees, I gained valuable experience with supporting teachers and strategic planning. Under the tutelage of highly effective leaders, I take advantage of the opportunity to build my capacity as a teacher leader.

During my tenure as a teacher, I was selected to my district's first Aspiring Leaders Program cohort. The cohort consisted of the top ten teacher leaders from around the district. During my program internship, I was tasked with performing a program evaluation of my district's school technology support model. My recommendations ultimately supported change within the district. This was a key experience that further fueled my desire to become an assistant principal.

Bambrick-Santoyo (2012) identifies seven core areas of school leadership, which are referred to as levers in the book *Leverage Leadership*: What experiences have you had as an assistant principal in each of the seven core areas identified?

Instructional Levers:

1. *Data-driven Instruction:* To streamline and further develop data-driven instructional practices, I played a role in revamping my school's assessment practices. In years' past, teachers were administering unit pre-assessments on day one of the respective unit and expected to utilize the data immediately. My school team found this to be an ineffective and somewhat unrealistic practice. This led to a decision to administer pre-assessments two weeks prior to the beginning of each unit. Teachers now have ample time to analyze the pre-assessment data and group students appropriately to differentiate instruction. I currently engage in data protocols with

content teams to analyze data, identify student misconceptions, and support with flexible grouping strategies.

2. *Observation and Feedback:* Face-to-face feedback meetings have been a staple of my Assistant Principal journey. I emphasize the use of accurate notes to engage teachers in feedback meetings that are geared toward specific action steps for improvement. My feedback meetings are also grounded in bite-sized feedback that can be applied immediately. I also focus on providing precise, positive reinforcement and praise as teachers complete action steps that are aligned to designated timelines.

    In order to get an accurate idea of my performance as an evaluator, I have instituted an anonymous evaluator feedback protocol to provide teachers with a voice. This gives teachers an opportunity to rate my performance and provide suggestions for my improvement as an evaluator.

3. *Instructional Planning:* Management of Professional Learning Communities (PLC) are integral to the support that I give to content teams. During the PLC meetings, I assist teams with using a backwards design framework. I have worked with key personnel to revise lesson plan templates to include an emphasis on differentiated instruction, rigor, and specific student learning objectives. My school is the first cohort of the district's personalized learning initiative. One component of this initiative is the development of instructional model that is geared toward instruction in digital environments.

    While creating our instructional model, I leaned on my elementary teaching experience to develop station rotation models that rely on ongoing formative assessments while target different learning styles.

4. *Professional Development:* I have led several professional development efforts on both the school and district level. I have crafted a professional development plan that is founded on taking a grassroots approach to transform instructional practices. Prior to each of professional development session, teachers take a pre-assessment on the content that will be covered during the upcoming session. I use that pre-assessment data to group teachers appropriately for differentiated activities.

Each professional development session requires teachers to engage in a performance task which gives me the opportunity to check for understanding. Completing the performance tasks is a valuable component of my professional development framework because it gives teachers the chance to practice before implementing the given strategy within their respective classrooms.

At the district level, I have facilitated professional development trainings for District and School Administrators. I have re-delivered personalized learning initiative trainings to other Assistant Principals. I have also collaborated with peers to develop the Innovative School Leader Academy which is designed to provide school administrators with a hands-on experience with Microsoft Office 365 tools. During these sessions, leaders explore Microsoft tools that can be used to enhance the production and performance of school leaders in 21st century learning environments.

My expertise with Microsoft education tools has elevated me to gain a national presence as educational technology trainer. As a result, I have facilitated Microsoft trainings during conferences and seminars in several states. Furthermore, I have gained experience with planning professional development conferences. As a Microsoft Showcase School leader, my school's administrative team is encouraged to host Redefining Learning Conferences. I served as a co-host at the largest school Redefining Learning Conference in U.S. History. The conference tallied over 1,200 participants and 130 presenters. The conference hosted attendees from across the district to engage in a full day of learning.

Culture Levers:

1. *Student Culture:* In the midst of my school's recent transition to 1:1 device initiative, I worked with school teams to build a student culture that is centered on digital citizenship. I have organized a student technology leadership team that successfully completed a three-day training program.

   This student team supports teachers and students with technical issues while serving as role models for their peers. In addition, all students have completed virtual simulations that are designed to guide students on BEST practices for technology use. This effort has led to our school being recognized as a Digital Citizenship certified school.

2. *Staff Culture:* As the eighth-grade Assistant Principal, I had full autonomy over the operations and procedures of the eighth-grade team. Prior to implementing procedures, routines, and protocols, I made a conscious effort to develop a shared mission and vision for the grade level while ensuring that student success was at the forefront of our goals. Teachers are given ample opportunities for frequent feedback through anonymous surveys and by maintaining an open-door policy.

   I also overemphasize the use of positive reinforcement and praise to help teachers feel appreciated for their efforts. More recently, I have incorporated a digital badging system for teachers. Teachers can earn points for various tasks that lead to a series of badges and incentives that the teachers can earn throughout the school year.

3. *Managing School Leadership Teams:* In addition to my role of Assistant Principal, I also serve as a regional lead for our district's instructional team. This position requires me to support and evaluate tech team members on the quality of the instructional technology support initiatives. Since most management is virtual, I provided a mixture of video technology and written communication to offer feedback and support. Our quarterly face-to-face meetings give me a chance to re-establish a rapport with team members.

What specific experiences in your tenure as an assistant principal have allowed you to increase your readiness to assume the role of principal?

My experience at all three levels of K-12 education (elementary, middle, and high) has given me a unique perspective background within the realm of school-based leadership. My origins as an elementary teacher have given me a solid instructional background with Understanding by Design frameworks. My high school experience as a Dean of Students has given me a plethora of experience with school management and operations.

My current role as a middle school Assistant Principal has allowed me to maximize my impact on teaching and learning practices. My focus on personalized learning has prepared me for the future of education and 21st century school environments. My principal has supported me in driving our paperless school initiative. The majority of my school's classrooms are facilitating instruction in a paperless environment. This initiative has required me to create an instructional plan, professional development plan, and communications plan that has impacted school-wide change. In years' past, secondary assistant principal roles have been categorized into the following three roles:

- Curriculum Assistant Principal-responsible for scheduling and teaching and learning
- Testing Assistant Principal-responsible for testing and teaching and learning
- Discipline Assistant Principal-responsible for discipline, operations, and school safety. I would like to humbly add a fourth dimension: The Technology Principal. My recent evolution into this role coupled

with my everlasting desire to grow has increased my readiness to become a 21st century principal.

In the book *Leadership Challenge,* Kouzes and Posner (2002) identify "Five Practices of Exemplary Leadership"

Choose one of the five practices and explain how you currently demonstrate that practice.

My current leadership practices are closely aligned with **Model the Way.** Technological competence is not necessarily a skill set that is stressed in the majority of undergraduate teacher preparation programs. Therefore, I feel that it is my obligation to model effective technology integration. In order to build the buy-in of the staff, I demonstrate how to leverage the tools while providing job-embedded professional development. This practice is evidenced in my approach to meeting teachers where they are and setting interim goals to build their capacity. Successful completion of small action steps allows me to gain "easy wins" with teachers. Once I build their confidence, it typically correlates into a positive impact on their technology-based instructional practices.

What activities and learning experiences do you recommend for assistant principals aspiring to assume the role of principal?

I strongly recommend that aspiring principals master a skill set in addition to becoming a jack-of-all-trades. For example, an Assistant Principal responsible for testing should master the testing process and also develop his/her capacity in areas of curriculum, discipline, professional development, operations, and technology. A well-rounded background and expertise in multiple areas of school leadership would be an advantage when stepping into the role of a principal. Current Assistant Principals should seek to gain behind-the-scenes experiences with school budgeting and community relations. Developing a positive rapport with key stakeholders is vital to building buy-in from the school community as a new principal.

I would also recommend seeking experience pairing up with a mentor at the district level. Completing an internship project or shadowing a district leader can offer a lens into the deeper inner-workings of district operations. Establishing a presence in a Professional Learning Network with school leaders working in similar settings would also serve as a benefit to aspiring principals.

What do you believe are five (5) key characteristics of effective leadership? Describe how you demonstrate each of those characteristics.

1. *GRIT Factor:* Effective leadership in the K-12 sector requires school leaders

to demonstrate "Grit." Grit takes common themes of work ethic and dedication exhibited by most leaders a step further by adding a sense of resilience and fortitude that is unparalleled with peers. In order to drive and cultivate innovation and overcome organizational obstacles, leaders must be willing to demonstrate an unswerving desire to achieve goals and meet the needs of students. I demonstrate grit while managing 1:1 device deployments and personalized learning initiative.

2. *Emotional Intelligence:* Developing a positive staff culture implores leaders to develop their ability to assess emotional behaviors to guide decision making and action steps. I lean on my emotional intelligence to discern the attitudes of staff members. I primarily use this skill to adjust my professional development sessions to cater to the emotions of the participants. I also use emotional intelligence to assess talent and leadership qualities of teacher leaders. When training our teacher leaders I stress the importance of remaining "emotionless" while conducting business and having critical conversations.

3. *Motive:* Historically, great leaders held a motive that ultimately led them to achieve success. I am firm believer that motive is a pre-determinant of GRIT. My motive to change the learning experience for students began when my fourth-grade teacher told me that I "don't look gifted." I have been on a mission to prove her wrong for the past 20 years. This eventually led to my decision to pursue a career in education. My demonstration of this characteristic is evidenced in my motivation to excel in multiple areas of school leadership. Becoming an Assistant Principal at the age of 27 speaks to my motive to lead.

4. *Poise:* Remaining calm under pressure is an indicator of an effective leader. When faced with challenges, I strive to maintain my composure and make decisions that are in the best interest of students. I also maintain poise when meeting with key stakeholders and interacting the local school community.

5. *Transparency:* I consciously work to maintain transparency with all students, teachers, and parents. I give stakeholders an opportunity to engage in open dialogue with me with the mutual expectation that I provide transparent answers. This practice has increased my access within my school, which has ultimately increased my reliability among the staff.

In the book *School Culture Rewired*, Steve Gruenert and Todd Whitaker (2015) explains the difference in school climate and school culture as the climate represents the weather today and school culture represents the weather over a long period of time (overall).

When you are appointed principal, how would you assess the current status of your new school's climate and culture? Identify the characteristics of a school with a positive climate and culture.

My immediate steps to assess the state of the school climate and culture would follow the sequence below:

1. Access state accountability performance assessment of the school climate
2. Access data and/or evidence of a student Positive Behavior Interventions and Supports (PBIS) system
3. Administer a student survey related to school culture
4. Administer a staff survey related to school culture
5. Administer a parent survey related school culture

A thorough analysis of the school's performance in the area of school climate and culture on the state performance assessment would give me insight on the current climate of the school as it relates to students, teachers, and parents.

To get an instant pulse on the climate of the school, I would analyze current practices with PBIS systems and routines. Consistent and effectively run PBIS programs typically correlate to a positive impact on school culture over time. I would place a heavy emphasis on administering surveys in an effort to gain valuable feedback from primary stakeholders.

The teacher survey questions would inquire about professional collaboration, Teacher Efficacy, and Administrative Support. The student survey would inquire about safety, learning environment, and motivation. The parent survey would contain questions about communication and parental involvement. Capturing data from these surveys would give me additional insight on stakeholder perceptions.

Three emerging characteristics of a school with a positive culture are Collaboration, Values, and Equity. Collaboration should be practiced between both students and teachers on key decisions that affect the student experience. Collaboration must also be present among teachers and administration. It is critical for administrators, teachers, and students to identify with a set of core values which outline the expectations for student and staff behavior and interactions. Equity must also be incorporated to ensure that all students feel supported and valued as students.

What educational leaders are saying about Darren A. Clay:

"Darren is reflective in his practice. He is not afraid to fail and try again. He has the ability to relate to a variety of stakeholders. The calculated risks he takes allow him to be innovative and unconventional in the approaches he takes with teachers and students. His withitness ensures that he is aware of what is taking place in his department, grade level, and immediate surroundings."

– Anthony Newbold, Ed.D., Current Supervisor

"Mr. Clay is a natural leader. He has the ability to keep his team focused on goals and meeting the needs of students."

Darren has been serving students from diverse backgrounds since August of 2011. Darren has enjoyed serving in multiple educational leadership roles at the K-12 and collegiate levels. In his current role, he has been highly involved with technology integration efforts as a Technology Assistant Principal at a Microsoft Showcase School.

Darren has led personalized learning efforts and launched 1:1 device initiatives. In addition, Darren facilitates the technology integration processes between teacher and student within Office 365 environments.

Over the past two years, Darren co-hosted the largest school-led Microsoft Redefining Learning Conference in U.S. history. He enjoys collaborating with showcase schools throughout the globe and continues to deliver job-embedded technology support to school leaders. As a regional technology team lead, Darren helps to drive technology innovation in over 20 schools.

Darren currently holds advanced degrees in Instructional Technology and Educational Leadership. As a current doctoral student at the University of Georgia, he studies technology integration in urban school settings.

Darren is globally recognized as a Microsoft Innovative Educator Expert, Microsoft Surface Expert, Microsoft Certified Educator and Microsoft Office Specialist. His expertise has given the opportunity to collaborate with Microsoft application product managers in Beijing. Darren received a national Whitney M. Young, Jr. Award from the Boy Scouts of America for his dedication and service to youth. Most recently, Darren was named Assistant Principal of the Year in his district's learning community.

His ultimate role is to give stakeholders an adequate opportunity to succeed with proven educational practices within 21st century learning environments.

"Before you can correct...you must connect"– Gary M. Clay, Sr.

Ursula A. Golladay

"There is accountability for everyone!" – *U. Golladay*

What motivated or inspired you to become an assistant principal?

Taking it way back, I am the oldest girl of five children and did a lot of "leading" from a very early age. While by far it is not the most "important" skill of leadership, multitasking is definitely something I mastered back then. That is also when I grew to love children. But, the truth is that working with people that are true leaders to me, people that inspired me to form great relationships with others, is what inspired me to become a leader myself. I was fortunate to work under many great "bosses." Bosses that were kind, bosses that were strict, bosses that were eccentric, terrible bosses; I learned to sort out what I liked, what did not inspire me and which great leadership qualities I wanted to emulate! The great ones always inspired me to work harder so that I could be a part of what they were doing. So that I too could have a hand in the growth and success.

Bambrick-Santoyo (2012) in *Leverage Leadership* identifies seven core areas of school leadership, which are referred to as levers. What experiences have you had as an assistant principal in each of the seven core areas identified?

As an assistant principal of a newly opened school, we had minimal data to work with - assessment data, that is. Because we lacked an abundant amount of results, it allowed us to really reflect on what was going on with our students and what direction we needed to take. We took a look at the standardized test scores, unit assessments, report card grades and classroom assignments and identified academic priorities and worked to ensure our teachers were literate in the assessments being given. This drove professional development choices and planned instruction. Which leads me to observation and feedback in the schoolhouse. 98% of my staff has had less than two years of experience teaching. Observing teachers in instruction, but also in collaborative planning and being a part of the conversation, has been very important. I have learned that it isn't necessary to insert myself into every conversation to have an impact, but to be aware of what is happening in the building and how that capacity for instruction or even just working together has been essential to my journey as an assistant principal.

I cannot speak enough about the work it takes to build culture within a school and how that culture affects results. As the founding assistant principal of a new school, we began with students imported from several different neighborhoods, a team of teachers with little to no teaching experience, and a leadership team that had never met before. I wanted to just make decisions and run with them, but I learned to wait, not to overwhelm staff and gradually let them come to learn what they might need from me. Learning what strengths and needs are in these various groups is important.

What specific experiences in your tenure as an assistant principal has allowed you to increase your readiness to assume the role of principal?

I am well aware that thinking I'm ready to be a principal and being the principal are two very different things. However, my principal/mentor has given me the opportunity to sit in on many different and difficult conversations. Multi-tasking and "managing" have always come easy to me, but handling issues with interpersonal relationships between various staff members has been something to learn. No matter how many systems you put in place, there is still room for human error. That one time a five year old gets off at the wrong bus stop and the mother calls the school frantically on a Friday at 4:00 p.m. is the worst!

I have learned to ask many questions and who to ask those questions to. I have learned that jumping in the car and driving to that mother's house speaks volumes to the parent and the community. In the end, the child has always been found, thank God, but it sure is a long wait.

In the book *Leadership Challenge,* Kouzes and Posner (2002) identify "Five Practices of Exemplary Leadership":

Out of the five practices of Exemplary Leadership, I choose the one, which I had to learn about the most. I think many leaders are able to make decisions, they are confident and capable, but they forget that they can't do it all on their own. I know that I will not be able to survive on my own - I need coworkers/colleagues to work through the problems and challenges that we face together so that we can come up with those solutions together. I want my colleagues to know that I care about them and what they bring to the table. I make it a point to pay attention to their suggestions during meetings, to read the minutes and schedule time to talk about their suggestions. I make it a point to support their departments to make sure that they succeed. Another important way that I have tried to enable others is to create a shared vision. Together, we discuss the various roles we will have in making our vision happen, there has been more buy in and they know what their role is in helping the vision come to fruition, they know to "act." Lastly, it is very important to me that my teammates know that there is accountability for everyone. They are aware that I am committed to the work I have signed on for and accountable to for getting it down - I will ALWAYS follow through. Through the practices that I have mentioned above, I have created an environment where my colleagues know that we are committed to the same things and they are willing to take a risk and "act" upon our vision.

What activities and learning experiences do you recommend for assistant principals aspiring to assume the role of principal?

One of the ways that I learn the most is through doing. I had a conversation with my principal about letting me become more involved. I wanted to sit in on the meetings so that I could learn and take notes, then, we set aside time to discuss what I thought. Through his feedback and my reflection, he felt increasingly more confident that I could do those jobs on my own. My principal also went out on paternity leave, this gave me the experience to be "in charge." This was an experience where I was the one that people turned to for answers - and there are a lot of questions. I was once told that being a principal was making lots of decisions throughout the day and that was so true!

What do you believe are five (5) key characteristics of effective leadership? Describe how you demonstrate each of those characteristics.

1. *Emotional Intelligence* – An important quality of a great school leader is Emotional Intelligence (EI). School leaders need to be trustworthy and honest by listening, telling the truth and being up-front with all stakeholders, teachers, parents and students. I make myself available for conversation every day. I listen and ask teachers about the things they have shared with me in previous conversations. This shows the teachers that I care. Effective leaders must have the ability to understand and manage their own emotions and to be able to recognize and manage the emotions of others. Reflecting on the decisions that I have made and the effects of those decisions through journaling have been a wonderful growth experience for me. I have to look at myself in the mirror every day and I always strive to be fair, have good manners, punctuality, etc., all the qualities that I ask of staff and students.

2.   *Be a Community Builder* – An effective school leader is a community builder. This leader will invest in developing strong teachers who are committed to the vision. Instead of being concerned with being "top dog", I realize they need high functioning teams and community that will be there for the school. I strive to find teachers in the school that want to be a part of "something bigger." I invite community partnerships into the building that will build on ideas that these teachers have shared with me. These relationships are important and enable staff to take ownership of the vision and feel motivated to follow through. Allowing these relationships shows that I trust others and in turn they will trust me; and that whether I am in the building or not, the vision will go on.

3.   *Be Visible* – To be effective a leader I position myself in the front of the building every single morning greeting as many students as possible. When arrival is over, instead of going into my office to tackle to mounds of paperwork I go into classrooms with substitutes, I check-in on my more needy students and ensure my newer teachers have gotten off to a great start for the day. Simply smiling at students and staff and saying hello in the hallways sets a tone of positivity for the day. Teachers know that I will be there if they need me and both staff and students are very used to seeing me in and around their classrooms. During observations and conferences you have to talk about instruction, it is a lot easier to talk with some background knowledge. If the teacher knows that you have been around and if this isn't the first time you've been in their classroom, they respect your opinion a great deal more.

4.   *Have a Vision and a Plan* – An effective leader is one that has a clear sense of where they are going and what their purpose is for being there. An effective visionary leader has a plan for students academically and socially and has worked with others to develop this plan. Whether it be disciplinary, putting a procedure or protocol into place or making the duty schedule, every decision I make revolves around the plan. If the vision for the school needs a champion, I am there to back it up.

5.   *Problem Solver* – While this title sounds like I solve every problem, I feel that an effective leader is able to empower her staff and students to solve problems. I can't always resolve every issue and usually gather a team to move forward. If an issue is brought to my attention, the first thing I do is think through the people that may be able to help find a solution to the problem. I am careful to remain calm and consider all options and, if

I am unable to solve the problem or make a bad decision, I am resilient, reflect on what when wrong and begin to put a plan into place for what should happen next time around.

In the book *School Culture Rewired*, Steve Gruenert and Todd Whitaker (2015) explains the difference in school climate and school culture as the climate represents the weather today and school culture represents the weather over a long period of time.

When you are appointed principal, how would you assess the current status of your new school's climate and culture? Identify the characteristics of a school with a positive climate and culture.

When I am appointed principal, I will need to know what my values and beliefs are and identify things that influence those values and beliefs. Throughout my tenure, I will commit to using a specific language to carry-out this mission. As a newly appointed principal to a school, I think it's important to identify what the school has done well, who has played a part in making those wins happen, and build on those successes. These are the specific people that might be willing to support our mission on creating a great school climate! It is important to spend time figuring out a baseline for where we are with certain concerns such as collegiality and their ability to collaborate with one another. I would want to know what professional development might be needed and whether we all have the same goal in mind. Once we have figured out what the most important needs are, I will have teachers think about ways we might address them and begin to plant the seeds of change. Using trusted teachers or staff members, I would ask them to help spread the seeds - and monitor the conversations and instructional moves throughout the year.

At the end of the year, I hope to be able to identify who the allies of our goals are and with these allies create a School Improvement team to spread the word. I know that this is not the end but instead a cyclical process that will need to be identified, monitored and modified again and again. The hope is to have a staff that feels as though their successes are celebrated and wants to collaborate with one another to build on those successes. I would like to have a staff that feels responsible for improving their own skills. In my school with a positive climate and culture, there is a consistent behavior policy and teachers are positive about their students. Learning environments are open and welcoming, child centered and individualized because teachers feel supported in their use of the curriculum and new ideas.

What educational leaders are saying about Ursula Golladay:

"I have had the pleasure of supervising Ms. Golladay's school and working with her for the past two and a half years. Ms. Golladay is an educator par excellence. She is at once a teacher, learner and leader. This practice is evident when observing Ms. Golladay provides professional development and support to school teams, in the process building the instructional capacity of teachers."

"Mrs. Golladay demonstrates a passion for teaching excellence, high-impact leadership, and community building. She is sensitive, flexible, respected and admired by students, parents, and colleagues alike. I am deeply impressed by her and recommend her without reservation. I am confident if selected for a position within our district, she would provide the same high level of service and commitment."

Ursula A. Golladay is a founding school Assistant Principal at an elementary school in Maryland. With fifteen years as an elementary school music teacher and three years as an assistant principal, Ursula Golladay brings a wealth of knowledge about educating the whole child through music and arts integration. Ursula Golladay has earned her Bachelor of Science in Choral/Vocal & General Music from the University of Maryland, College Park and her Masters in Educational Leadership from Hood College with endorsements for Administration I & II.

As an educational leader, Ursula has focused on nurturing an instructional program that values learning as a process wherein there will be trials and errors, and that together with peers, teachers, and family every student is expected to explore his or her own sense of self while developing tools to reflect and seek healthy independence. Under Ursula's leadership, Title I students have gained an understanding of their "whole" self through an arts integrated approach. This approach has provided a foundation for individual development that ultimately, undeniably, has benefited society and individual citizenship. Mrs. Golladay has brought this vision to fruition through grants and has co-written and been awarded in studies such as Japanese Arts & Music and the study of African American History.

21st century education embodies an approach to teaching and learning that positively supports schools as communities where all students can learn at high levels because of students' differences. Under Mrs. Golladay's care, her school is a place that nurtures growth in all members of the community and has taken her current school's volunteerism from three parent volunteers to 85 volunteers. She has provided nights for fingerprinting and worked hard to find ways to involve parents in their children's education. To Mrs. Golladay, effort is rewarded with self-confidence and commitment and is held with the highest regard. Ms. Golladay encourages diversity in her field and in her teachers, having studied and taught in Japan and several places in the diverse Washington, D.C. area.

Ursula excels in setting up school structure and management having co-chaired the school district's Scheduling Committee and presented documents to the Labor Management Committee. She has also managed the school district's Middle School Honors Choruses. In addition to management, Ursula is passionate about developing curriculum and has co-written the district's Curriculum 2.0 Enduring Understandings for General Music. Rounding out her goals, Ursula Golladay currently serves on the Board of Trustees for Feynman School in Bethesda, Maryland a school for children gifted in science and math.

On the weekends, you'll find Ursula singing as the lead soprano in a local choir and spending time with her husband and two children, which are her heart. Her family keeps her focused on what's important in every part of her life – family and developing children into the kind of people who contribute globally to the world around us.

"If your actions inspire others to dream more, learn more, do more and become more, you are a leader." – John Quincy Adams

LeCinda R. Jennings

"The process of planning professional development contributed to my own growth as an instructional leader." – L. Jennings

What motivated or inspired you to become an assistant principal?

As a young child, I experienced some struggles in school. These struggles were not academic, social, or physical in nature, but developed as a result of my response to a teaching style. Academics had never been an issue with me. I soared academically. Very often, I was one of the first, if not the first, to complete my assignments with perfect or near perfect accuracy. School work was a breeze for me. However, my teacher was ill equipped to accommodate this fact. As soon as I completed one assignment, I can remember another assignment being given to keep me "busy." As a result, I became restless as I came to the realization that more work did not equal engaging work. I was compliant yet oftentimes begrudgingly so.

Despite the rebellion displayed in my behavior, I thrived academically. My school principal often celebrated students with praise and small treats.. He always celebrated my accomplishments, as I was a permanent fixture on the honor roll despite my behavior. I can recall going to his office to receive pencils, stickers, buttons, and praise from him. Little did I know, he was also reflecting on possible triggers for my disengagement. Through his insistence, I was eventually tested and identified to participate in the gifted and talented program in my school district. Gone were the back-to-back assignments to keep me busy and out of trouble. They were replaced by challenging assignments with more than one answer that caused me to use problem-solving skills, work collaboratively, and extend learning. From that time, I fell in love with school, the complexities of learning, and the healthy challenges I faced as a part of the gifted track.

To this day, I hold that principal in high regard because he saw past the behaviors that masked my frustrations thus helping me to thrive. I went on to graduate high school with college credit and I link this in part to a caring school administrator who took the time to think about how to help a little brown girl who did not know how to express her frustrations properly. After entering the field of education and teaching for several years, I decided that I wanted to be my own version of that administrator to students. As a bonus, I have the privilege to coach teachers, grow leaders, and further develop my own leadership skills.

Bambrick-Santoyo (2012) in *Leverage Leadership* identifies seven core areas of school leadership, which are referred to as levers. What experiences have you had as an assistant principal in each of the seven core areas identified?

Instructional Levers:

I have had the privilege to participate in experiences in each of the seven core areas identified in *Leverage Leadership* (Bambrick-Santoyo, 2012). In data-driven instruction, I have had the opportunity to analyze data to determine strengths and weaknesses of instruction, content areas, and the school and set goals for teaching and learning. In addition, I have been able to compare and contrast data for various programs to determine the effectiveness of programs on student learning and growth.

As a state certified mentor and evaluator, I provide observations, both formal and informal with direct feedback to teachers. As such, there are times I observe not as an evaluator but as a coach. This process takes finesse as the role of a coach serves as different purpose than that of an evaluator. However, both roles involve a level of trust that must be established and nurtured. In addition, I serve as the co-chair on evaluation teams for new and induction teachers. For veteran teachers, I collaborate to develop yearly goals and objectives, professional development areas, and when necessary design growth and competency plans.. This involves meeting with teachers at the beginning, middle, and year-end to assess progress toward goals and reflect on future areas of emphasis. In order to effectively develop goals, I have to perform as a competent team member in the instructional planning process.

As a former English-language arts teacher, my strength lies in reading and writing instruction. However, as an elementary assistant principal I had to expand my content knowledge to include the areas of science, math, and social studies. This does not mean that I have become an expert in all areas. On the contrary, I have had to use resources to aid me as an instructional planner. Some of the resources I regularly employ are those of the content specialists in my district. I am a part of a leadership team that does not hesitate to call upon these men and women to help me work through planning and to draw upon their vast knowledge base to guide me in guiding teachers. Quite naturally, I call upon these experts to assist me in locating and developing meaningful professional development experiences for teachers based on data, observations, and evaluations.

Cultural Levers:

I have most contributed to student culture through the creation of mentoring programs and the daily interactions I have with my students. In addition to discipline, I am committed to spending valuable time with those students who are successful in their behavior managements and academic achievement. I interact with students and parents at assemblies, extracurricular events and activities, as well as secure services to help students to be successful. I visit classrooms, co-teach, and attend field studies in order to ensure stakeholders and most importantly students understand that I care about the total child. Especially during discipline discussions, I use conversations and conferences as an opportunity to teach character, make connections, and encourage.

Teachers need to feel supported in discipline. They need to feel that they are included in decisions and that their input is both welcome and vital. I work closely with teachers and other staff members and make sure to give them credit individually and publicly for their efforts. In addition, the administrative team works diligently to conduct "pulse checks." These checks assess the climate, and provide an opportunity for the leadership team to inject opportunities for stress busters and support when it is most needed. In order to accomplish this we meet regularly to stay abreast of upcoming events, initiatives, data, technology use and instruction, character education, and other administrative responsibilities. The leadership team collaborates, brainstorms and shares the workload to ensure that the school functions as an excellent system of individuals with common goals and objectives. In the absence of my principal, I facilitate leadership team meetings. In his presence, I lead initiatives or simply participate as an active team member.

What specific experiences in your tenure as an assistant principal have allowed you to increase your readiness to assume the role of principal?

There have been several experiences in my tenure as an assistant principal that have assisted me in increasing my readiness to assume the role of principal. Specifically, there are three roles that have most allowed me to increase my readiness to assume the role of principal by providing me with valuable experiences.

Firstly, participation in the hiring process has provided me with the opportunity to personally select candidates for specific positions. In the selection process, I have had to not only identify the needs of the school, but also the needs of the team or department to determine to best fit for a position.. During the interview process, I have had the opportunity to ask questions and make observations that are tailored to the needs of each position. Although, the questions may differ depending on the position, participation in the hiring process has also developed a connection with applicants. I want to see them succeed and go above and beyond to participate as a coach and evaluator in order to provide intentional, effective feedback for growth. Additionally, I am committed to growing them as leaders in their own areas of strength. Principals know they cannot accomplish the goals of the learning organization on their own. Therefore it is crucial that they attract, retain, and develop the right talent to assist them.

Secondly, planning professional development has been a natural progression. In coaching teachers, both novice and veteran, it is necessary to determine the needs of individuals and groups. In order to effectively plan for meaningful professional development, I have had to gauge the needs of faculty and function as an instructional leader. I have had to focus on the development of my own skills of listening, reflecting, and data analysis and grow in these areas..

The process of planning professional development not only helped faculty to grow, but it simultaneously contributed to my own growth as an instructional leader.

One of my favorite opportunities for professional development involved delving into the project-based learning, or PBL, arena. As a school we decided to increase our understanding and all interested faculty attended professional development together. This training took place over several days during the summer. These daylong sessions provided the administrators, new teachers, and veteran teachers the opportunity to learn and work together. Connections and relationships were built as we all learned side by side. We learned new knowledge as well as reflected on prior knowledge to develop our skills for a different work. The work was engaging and fulfilling because we were all working toward a common goal that has been proven to be a benefit to children. Principals have to build relationships with other faculty members. It is nearly impossible to lead teachers to a new endeavor if they do not feel and believe that you are prepared and willing to roll up your sleeves and work beside them.

Lastly, I have served as the administrator in charge of facilities. There are so many duties and responsibilities that fall under this umbrella that are vital to the day-to-day operations of a school. One such responsibility is serving as the safety representative. In this role I am required to inspect the school regularly for safety measures. In addition, I promote the safety of all stakeholders while on campus. Specifically, recently my school replaced and updated the entire fire alarm system. I attended meetings with state and district facilities personnel, contractors, and subcontractors in order to ensure that the project was completed in its entirety. This project extended to well over a year and involved some construction while school was in session. I learned so much through this endeavor that enabled me to learn about school facilities at the local, district, and state level. As a principal, you are the representative for your school and it is ultimately your responsibility to know the intricate details in order to be proactive with the infrastructure and safety of your school.

In the book Leadership Challenge, Kouzes and Posner (2002) identify "Five Practices of Exemplary Leadership":

Choose one of the five practices and explain how you currently demonstrate that practice.

Challenge the Process

There are times when leaders get stuck in a rut, and fall in simply going along with what is comfortable and causes the least amount of ripples in the water. They may realize that the effectiveness of past initiatives has waned but they do not want to step into unchartered waters. Admittedly, the process of analyzing the effectiveness of a program can be daunting. In contrast, I enjoy the practice of challenging the process.

I came into an administrative position at a school that had seen little to no change in administration for some time. There were school events and practices that were in place because they had "always been done that way." Initially, I simply observed as there was so much to learn in my new position about the school, faculty members, and culture. Additionally, there was a period of time that involved building trust with all stakeholders. I used this period to make purposeful observations and take note of resources that may be required. Approaching the end of my first year as an assistant principal, I began asking questions and making suggestions. All of my suggestions were not explored nor met with open mindedness. My intention was not to offend, but at times offense was taken. I did not take this personally as these feelings often arose as a result of the possibility of change. This is all a part of the change process. As a leader, I understand human response is at times resistant to change. I accepted that some simply needed more time, but I did not allow this to halt progress. Patience is a key virtue during this stage of the change process.

One such project involved beginning a mentoring group specifically geared towards boys. From the data that was available I knew that boys were receiving an overwhelming majority of the discipline referrals. In addition, the school did not have an active boys mentoring program in place. To begin this venture, I joined the district mentoring steering committee as one of my first steps to learn the district's goals and objectives for all of its mentoring programs. As an administrator, I wanted to be involved in the process, but knew from experience the unpredictable nature of the duties that the position entailed. As such, I invited a male teacher with previous mentoring experience whom I believed possesses the attributes necessary to facilitate a successful program. Together, we stepped into the unknown and began our own mentoring program.

K.I.N.G.S. (Kind Intelligent Noble Gentlemen Students) was born and continues to thrive. Boys selected for the program meet regularly for fellowship, bonding, and mentoring opportunities. They have the opportunity to earn points daily for attendance, academics, and behavior and are rewarded for their efforts. Referrals are down and boys know they have access to mentors who care about their total well-being. Each quarter, boys who meet their goal participate in a group celebration. Past celebrations have included movie nights, free time on a traveling game bus, after school football games and grilling, and attendance at an NBA basketball game. The K.I.N.G.S. boys mentoring program has grown to be well respected and students who participate in the program have represented the school in several endeavors. I am proud of myself for challenging the process, and equally proud to see so many students' lives impacted.

Challenging the process involves taking risks with the realization that you may fall and mistakes will be made. However, there are always lessons in the mistakes, and the opportunity to hone leadership skills. Each experience builds the foundation for the next, which can all work together for your benefit.

What activities and learning experiences do you recommend for assistant principals aspiring to assume the role of principal?

Throughout my tenure as an assistant principal, I have learned that it is vital to my personal and professional growth to develop a professional growth plan. One major component of a professional growth plan involved securing a mentor. For this reason, I encourage those with aspirations to invest time in securing an effective mentor who has previously served in the role of principal. Aspiring principals would benefit from working closely with a mentor who will be able to serve as a sounding board, a trusted advisor, and give constructive feedback. Just as teachers have social, emotional, physical, and instructional needs, administrators have similar needs. An effective mentor is one who can provide a realistic idea of the many complexities that the role of principal entails.

Most importantly, an effective mentor will coach you in areas of strengths and weaknesses, which will ultimately help you to map out goals and objectives for your tenure as an administrator. As you map goals and objectives, you are better able to make decisions that allow you to chart your own path as an administrator. Find someone who possesses the qualities you admire and allow that person to help you to develop your own qualities while networking in the field. In addition, I encourage those aspiring to become principals to simply converse regularly with your own principal. Your direct supervisor will be able to provide you with unmatched advice and resources to other learning experiences that are highly recommended. Aspiring administrators should also be involved and participate on various committees and initiatives at the district level. It is important that you take an interest in not only your school, but also the district as a whole. In order to successfully have a perspective of the big picture, assistant principals need to leave the walls of their schools and participate in professional development, committees, and roles that allow them to network as well as be exposed to the community at large. Assistant principals who desire to work as principals have to shift from the mindset of trying to fix it all, and focus on building systems that support the development of teaching, learning of students, and maintenance of facilities.

Finally, and most importantly, I encourage those who have a desire to assume the role of principal to continue to teach. Often daily administrative duties route assistant principals away from what is most important as they become heavily engaged in the management aspects of the "books, buses, and behinds." For example, I suggest co-teaching with a teacher during a specific content area. Take the time to prepare a lesson with teachers, or serve as an assistant for the day. These experiences serve not only to remind you of the time and effort that is invested by your faculty each day, but also serve as a reminder for what is at the core of education and what should drive all that you implement, direct, and the decisions you make—teaching and learning.

What do you believe are five (5) key characteristics of effective leadership? Describe how you demonstrate each of those characteristics.

It is difficult to narrow down five characteristics of effective leadership. However, five characteristics of effective leadership that I believe most leaders possess are the following: risk takers, visionary, flexible, confidence, and good judgment.

I returned to my childhood hometown in the fall of 2007and served as teacher leader and department chair for five years. I knew in my heart of hearts that it was time for me to take my career to the next level and I was interested in leadership. I arranged a face-to-face meeting with the Director of Personnel to discuss my aspirations and future in the district. Although the Director spoke very highly of me, and her beliefs about my ability to lead, I walked away with the realization that there simply were no available positions in the small school district. Not having a desire to wait for a position to become available, I made the decision to change my address and move to another school district and city with more opportunities. I wrote down my goals and began to aggressively pursue them.

Two weeks later, I had secured a new position in a new city, district and school. During my first year, I learned of an opportunity to apply for a highly competitive leadership developmental program within the district. Despite admonitions from new colleagues about the competitive nature of the program, coupled with my fact that I had only been in the district for a couple of months, I decided to apply. As such, I was accepted into the program, took advantage of every opportunity to learn more about the culture of the district, and secured an administrator position within another year. Taking risks involves coming to the realization that the possibilities of failure are real, but they are outweighed by the potential for success.

In the book *School Culture Rewired*, Steve Gruenert and Todd Whitaker (2015) explains the difference in school climate and school culture as the climate represents the weather today and school culture represents the weather over a long period of time (overall).

When you are appointed principal, how would you assess the current status of your new school's climate and culture? Identify the characteristics of a school with a positive climate and culture.

There are a variety of ways a new principal can assess the climate and culture of a school. Initially, I would seek to observe the interactions of stakeholders at the school level. These observations would take place at various times of the day. For example, during the busy lunch hours, during arrival and dismissal times, during faculty meetings, at a parent teacher association meeting, and on the playground. Additionally, I would seek to conduct brief one-on-one interviews with each member of the staff at the school as an informal meeting to introduce myself and learn something about my new team members.

I would also seek to assess the climate by conducting surveys to give me data to effectively analyze and allow me to assess major factors such as teaching and learning, relationships, and safety. These surveys would be administered to students, parents, faculty, and staff. I would aim to visit meetings with the Parent Teacher Organization and/or School Improvement Council, not as a participant but as an observer.

In observing and collecting data, I understand that schools with a positive climate and culture are not accidental, perfect or without challenges. Schools with a positive climate and culture may have stakeholders with different opinions, but all stakeholders are committed to accomplishing the same goal. Although stakeholders may have different opinions they focus on what is best for reaching the goals and objectives set forth by all. In addition, schools with a positive climate and culture are committed to collaborating and continual growth. Leadership teams dismantle the "us versus them" mentality and empower others to serve as innovators. One such example stems from my current elementary school where the cafeteria manager began a cooking club. Students were taught how to prepare healthy and tasty meals. As a result, the club popularity and success of the cooking club grew with students, faculty, and parents. The cafeteria manager applied for an innovation grant that was offered by the school district. Her idea for a cooking show was accepted and funded providing a broader audience and providing positive exposure for all. This is an example of how a positive school climate and culture work to empower all stakeholders and impact student success.

What educational leaders are saying about LeCinda Jennings:

Ms. Jennings is a confident leader who has a strong desire to continue to learn about what it takes to be a school leader.

My own view is that that you will find it difficult to identify a candidate who combines so seamlessly LeCinda's teaching and leadership experience, her passion for helping those in need and her personal integrity.

LeCinda has over 17 years of experience as a teacher and administrator in South Carolina's public schools. Throughout her career she has remained a committed and serious lifelong learner. The evidence of this is in her impressive list of career accomplishments, certificates and advanced degrees.

Courageous, passionate, and self-aware are words used to describe LeCinda Jennings. In addition to her vibrant personality, LeCinda's transformational leadership style in teaching and learning, along with a compelling sense of self-efficacy all make her an excellent candidate for Principalship.

LeCinda has had the privilege to work as a school administrative assistant, classroom teacher, department chair, and assistant principal. A proud military veteran, she has mastered the art of self-discipline to accomplish tasks effectively and efficiently. She takes pride in the hiring of those who possess the same passion for children that she holds. In addition, one of her goals as a leader is to continue to develop and retain excellent teachers through coaching and effective feedback for growth. In addition, LeCinda enjoys helping teachers to grow as teacher-leaders by providing opportunities for both professional and personal development.

With a heart for mentoring, LeCinda currently serves on her district's mentoring steering committee. She is an advocate for all children and finds pleasure in serving students from various backgrounds. However, she has an exceptional gift for working with those students who experience structural difficulties by providing interventions and pathways for them to successfully navigate despite difficulties they may face. LeCinda has a commitment to working together with students, families, communities, and other stakeholders to provide students with a solid foundation for learning.

Additionally, LeCinda's educational gifts extend into the community at large via her own non-profit organization. She is the CEO and Founder of Girls of Leadership and Distinction Incorporated, (G.O.L.D.), a 501(c) (3) organization that inspires girls of today to flourish into strong, smart, and bold leaders of the future. Since 2007 G.O.L.D. has successfully served over 250 girls and young ladies through exposure to service learning, goal-setting, academic initiatives, and college and career readiness skills.

LeCinda believes that children are one of our most valuable resources, and the most masterful educational leaders are those who show a genuine commitment to lifelong teaching and learning. She aspires to inspire students and teachers to develop self-confidence, critical thinking skills, and compassion for others while accomplishing the goals of the classroom, school, and district. LeCinda knows that today's students are tomorrow's leaders and these characteristics are essential to successfully navigate and positively impact our diverse world.

"Aspire to inspire before you expire." – Eugene Bell, Jr.

Natasha McDonald

"Servant leadership takes you far." – N. McDonald

What motivated or inspired you to become an Assistant Principal?

The principal who hired me to be a first year teacher inspired me to become an assistant principal. He did walk-throughs and observations in my ELA classroom and he started planting the seed during my third year as a teacher. I was not thinking about leaving the classroom because I loved teaching so much, but he was persistent, and he kept telling about the increased impact I'd have on students. I finally enrolled in graduate school and when I finished, he hired me to be his Assistant Principal the following school year. We worked together as an admin team for one year and then he retired. Although I was completely devastated with the news of his retirement, I am thankful that he saw something in me that I did not see in myself. That is part of great leadership; helping others to tap into unseen potential and exceed expectations they have for themselves.

Bambrick-Santoyo (2012) in *Leverage Leadership* identifies seven core areas of school leadership, which are referred to as levers: What experiences have you had as an assistant principal in each of the seven core areas identified?

Instructional Levers:

I was fortunate to serve as an Academic Dean of Instruction for three years on a middle school campus. In that role, I was responsible for all things teaching and learning. Our district implemented professional learning communities and we met daily in core groups. We worked around four questions.

The meetings took varied forms depending on what was needed. Teachers collaborated and planned exciting lessons, they unpacked the student expectations to ensure everyone on the team was aligned in what would be presented to students, they analyzed student work samples and looked and what went well and what needed improvement. They also created common formative assessments and looked explicitly at the data, and modeled mini lessons.

Over time, we also created a system for helping teachers to look at their data by class, by grade level teams and we were able to drill down to individual students. We found that many times, people collected data and did nothing with it, so we decided to be intentional about creating a data process that answered the question, "What are we going to do about it." For more information on data, please watch the video that I created a few years ago for my staff. http://screencast-o-matic.com/watch/c2XFIQeFyy

In Texas, we have recently changed our Teacher Evaluation system from the Professional Development and Appraisal System (PDAS), to the Texas Teacher Evaluation and Support System (T-TESS). I was part of a pilot district and found the new appraisal system to be very time consuming, but when done with fidelity, extremely impactful. For the first time ever, we do pre-conferences with teachers where we talk about what they will be teaching, then conduct the observation where the administrator scripts everything that is happening during the lesson, and conduct a post conference to talk about areas of reinforcement and refinement prior to giving out a rating. There is also a goal-setting component that suggests that everyone has room for growth, and this aligns well with the growth mindset.

Our campus was very intentional about the kinds of professional development that was brought to our campus. There were times that we conducted whole staff professional development based on campus needs, i.e. True Colors and Champs, to help build relational capacity for the staff and also to have a unified discipline management system. At other times, professional development took place during PLC for different departments based on the needs of that department. As an instructional leader, I also provided flipped classrooms for the teachers when it was necessary to teach them something and we used the time during PLC to talk about it and they watched the videos outside of PLC.

Cultural Levers:

In my experience, I have found that it is quite difficult to impact cultural levers. I was an Assistant Principal on the same campus that I was an Academic Dean of Instruction. My first year on the campus, my principal charged me with finding a way to positively impact student culture. I borrowed an idea from a previous co-worker, with his blessings of course, and created a school store incentive. I made the school money and gave each teacher a monthly budget with a charge of celebrating more of what they want to see. I wrote letters to businesses and got donations for our students and the students were able to use their money one Friday a month at the school store on "Friday Buy Day." The students loved it. The school store helped build a positive rapport between the staff and the students. It also created a way to celebrate students who were not normally celebrated. When our stockpile got low, I sent an email to our parents asking for donations and we were pleasantly surprised to get such a positive response. We even had members of the PTA personally come to work the school store each month.

During those years, we also realized that our students lacked school pride. We worked together as a leadership team to make immediate changes. We decided to divide and conquer. My team and I took on the social media/website, and the principal and her team took on campus beautification. The results were amazing. We started tweeting, updating Facebook, and displaying student pictures on our website. I was at an open enrollment school district where students were given choice to select the campus they wanted to attend and we had several students and parents who showed interest based on our social media influence.

On the same campus, there were three different principals in a span of four years, all with very different leadership styles. The first principal was a very spontaneous and an out of the box thinker, the second was a leader who was skilled at building relationships and the third was a deep analytical thinker that asked tons of questions and was intentional about knowing the "why" behind everything that we did to ensure that it was all tied to student achievement. With all of the changes in leadership, it was definitely necessary to rebuild trust and relational capacity with the staff. We noticed the need during the transition from the second and third principal and decided to bring True Colors to our staff. The professional development was one of the best ones that I have had to date. It was relevant and teachers found it useful not only in their professional lives, but also in their personal lives. We were intentional about making sure the teachers knew that they were not learning about their color to use it as an excuse, but rather to learn ways to communicate with people who are not the same color, those who don't share personality traits. It helped the staff realize that the current principal was not a micromanager, but rather her "green" trait left her empty if she did not have a clear answer to the why we were doing what we were doing, and the impact it would have on student achievement. Our leadership team grew a very strong bond that year, and while most of us are at different campuses in different districts, we still keep in close communication with each other.

In addition to True Colors, we worked extremely hard to build relational capacity with the staff to impact school culture. I read a book called *Transforming School Culture* by Anthony Muhammad. The book made it really easy to put the teachers in one of four categories in order to strategize. They were the believers, tweeners, fundamentalist and survivors. This helped a great deal because I spent 80% of my days in PLC with different content areas and the book gave me effective strategies to work with staff members depending on which group they identified with. The following year, our leadership team attended professional development on Crucial Conversations. We practiced on each other and also with our accountability partners from training and rolled up our sleeves and did the work. Within that same school year, we became skilled in having difficult but necessary conversations to push our campus in the right direction. We were intentional about celebrations each month and worked to create a family like atmosphere. The majority of the staff welcomed the changes and followed our lead. There were a handful of staff members that were not on board and they chose to depart ways.

What specific experiences in your tenure as an assistant principal have allowed you to increase your readiness to assume the role of principal?

Campus Administrators wear several hats on a daily basis. We find ourselves mediating between teachers and students, parents and teachers, teachers and teachers, students and parents, co- parenting situations, you name it, I am sure we all have a plethora of stories to tell. Often times, I have found that the angry person really just wants to be heard. Allow them time to vent and get it out, within limits of course. Don't interrupt or attempt to talk over them as it only adds fuel to the fire and becomes a diversion from the real issue.

One year, I had to take my principal's place in a litigation Admission, Review and Dismissal process (ARD) meeting that lasted several days. During the time, it felt like a death sentence. Prior to that point in my career, I hadn't realized how quickly the hard work of our staff members could be used against them if they did not keep fine tooth documentation. This situation was very intense, but we grew closer as a campus because of it. Trials definitely build relational capacity. The teachers became advocates for effective documenta-tion and helped to create systems that worked and they were able to get other teachers to buy in.

Student conflict resolution comes very naturally and easy for me, but I had to learn how to skillfully manage adult conflict as I matured in my lead-ership. At one point, I had two teachers who were on the same team who were friends, and then something happened and they were instant enemies. They refused to plan together, one attempted to have arguments and drag other members of the department into the arguments, it definitely got ugly before it got better. I conducted what I call a "lemon squeeze" and allowed them to get their issues out on the table in a safe setting. I then reminded them of the social contract our team created at the beginning of the school year and one of the questions it asked was, "How do you want to be treated in times of conflict?" One of the main responses to that question was like a professional and also to have colleagues presume positive intent. We talked through that together. I also showed them their data on the district's common formative assessments. They went from being in the top half while collaborating together to landing in the bottom half while working in isolation. They didn't realize that they needed each other for the success of their students. Each one of them brought something valuable to the team. They absolutely did not walk away best friends, but they did walk away with a willingness to work together for the sake of the students.

I have learned a few things as I have matured in my leadership:

1. Keep a level head.
2. Don't make emotional decisions.
3. A decision does not necessarily have to be made today, but rather allow think time and time to confer with teammates if necessary.
4. Every child deserves due process.
5. Sometimes the teacher really does make a bad choice, investigate and help to resolve conflict in a timely fashion.
6. Apologize on behalf of the organization when necessary.
7. Don't take things personal when people are angry; nine out of ten times, you are not the target.
8. Be clear with your expectations and ensure your staff knows what is tight and what is loose.
9. Visit what you value.
10. Presume positive intent.
11. Document, Document, Document.
12. You must first be accountable before holding someone else accountable... as a leader, people watch and will do as you do, not as you say.
13. Servant leadership takes you far.
14. Relational Capacity can make or break an organization! People don't care how much you know until they know how much you care "Flippen Leadership"
15. The golden rule is golden. Treat students, staff, community members, parents and all stakeholders how you want you or your family to be treated.

In the book *Leadership Challenge*, Kouzes and Posner (2002) identify "Five Practices of Exemplary Leadership". Choose one of the five practices and explain how you currently demonstrate that practice.

Model the Way

This school year, I am in a new school district that has recently begun their journey in Professional Learning Communities. I came from a district that was six years into the process. Part of the change process is building relational capacity and trust amongst the staff. I add value to our team because I believe in the process 100% as I have seen it do miraculous things for student achievement, and that is my number one reason for being an educator. I worked with a reluctant department to create a social contract. Some people call it setting norms, but I think the social contract from the Flippen Leadership model of Capturing Kid's Hearts really does set a solid foundation for how we will conduct our business. As a team, we collaborated and came up with adjectives the following questions:

1. How do you want to be treated by administration?
2. How do you want to be treated by your colleagues?
3. How do you think administration wants to be treated by you?
4. How do we want to treat each other when there is conflict?

After our discussion, we created a document with all of the things that we all agreed upon and everyone signed it. As the training suggests, the document stays in the meeting room at all times. When I asked them for feedback on the process, they told me that is was the first time they had ever been asked those types of questions and they appreciated it. One of my favorite questions is number four because as well all know, it's ok until it's not ok. My team came up with presume positive intent. That was powerful. We revisit our social contract in individual and group settings and understand that we must hold each other accountable.

We followed the Capturing Kid's Hearts model and elected not to discuss our norms at each meeting as that can become mundane and no longer have value. Instead, we have started to follow the Xcel Model and at the start of each meeting, we ask for a volunteer to be a rater and an affirmer. At the end of the meeting, the rater will give our team an honest rating from 1-10 based on how we adhered to our commitments to one another. For example, almost every time I have created a social contract, respect of time is mentioned. If there is a meeting where there are multiple side bar conversations, a rater might say "I will rate us a 7 today because we had a lot going on. We were not necessarily good stewards of our time and could have been a bit more respectful to our presenter and we are better than that... we are shooting for a 10 next meeting." To ensure that we end the meeting on a positive note prior to launching, the person who volunteered to affirm will say something positive that is genuine. Immediately after, we launch them and the meeting is adjourned. Walking into a new district that is new to the process, I chose to Model the Way.

What activities and learning experiences do you recommend for assistant principals aspiring to assume the role of principal?

I would suggest that anyone who is aspiring to be a campus principal commit to being an instructional leader. Long gone are the days when Administrators presence on a campus is limited to meetings, discipline and evaluations. You must be competent, compassionate and capable. I would also suggest that an aspiring principal spend time learning all aspects of school. I have seen a few people skip the assistant principal role and go straight to being a campus principal, and it did not end well for many of the colleagues that I know. The assistant principal job is the best on the job training you can get. You are the heartbeat to the success of a school, and the eyes and ears that seem to be everywhere and know everything. As an assistant principal, you should always have something to do. Spend time in common planning meetings. Ask your principal if you can sit in on discussions with them and the secretary about the campus budget. Ensure you know how to create a master schedule, and that can get really tricky with singletons, double blocked classes and common planning requirements. Find a mentor, someone you can trust, who is successful and has longevity. Also find someone who is new to the role just like you so that you can celebrate together and freak out together. I like to call them my midnight buddy...someone who will pick up no matter what and help talk you off the ledge when you need it. Also work to find your balance. Your family should not be neglected continuously. You must sow seeds to find your rhythm, but you also need to have an accountability buddy to remind you that it is ok to shut it off, and not everything demands an immediate response. Have grace for yourself. Perfection is an enemy of the growth mindset.

What do you believe are five (5) key characteristics of effective leadership? Describe how you demonstrate each of those characteristics.

1. *Relational Capacity* – I value relational capacity because I believe in the power of creating an environment where people want to be. We spend over nine to ten hours a day together in the same building. We need to take time to ask about people's family, encourage a co-worker who is going through a difficult time, and hold those accountable who drag the team down. This is done through daily interactions and it must be genuine. If you are not a nurturing person, find someone who is and get them to hold you accountable. Block off the first 15 minutes of your day to walk a certain part of the building, randomly and get to know your staff.

2. *Address my own personal constraints daily* – In the Flippen Leadership Training, we learned that an organization cannot rise above the constraints of their leader and the organization with the least constraints wins. If you are choosing to lead, you must choose to address your own personal constraints. For example, I have a high need for order and structure. I have to be sure not to dominate and to give my staff autonomy on things that are loose and boundaries on things that are tight. My dominant color is gold on the True Colors test. With that, I am very task oriented, organized, etc. The not so great side of people who are gold can be that the task is viewed as more important than the person or that almost right is wrong, so it can be viewed as very controlling. I keep those things in mind when interacting with others to be sure that I keep them in check. Again, I have an accountability partner that I can call and crack up laughing or scream my head off and she does the same for me.

3. *Servant Leadership* – I have lived by the standard of not asking people to do things that I am unwilling to do. During cafeteria duty, I clean tables alongside the custodial staff. I have played school nurse when necessary, and even combed children's hair. My motto has always been, "Whatever it takes for student achievement, count me in!" I pick up paper in the hallways, teach classes when we are short on subs, mentor students who are in need, mentor staff members who are in need. I grade papers when teachers are stressed to the max, send cards of encouragement and just work to let people know that the job that we do as educators is the toughest yet most rewarding job ever. The little things go a long way.

4. *Clear vision and expectations* – With leadership, clear expectations and vision are very important. I am transparent with my staff as much as I

can be. At a previous campus, I implemented something called MYOD. It stands for My decision, Your decision, and Our Decision. The staff know that most of the time it was and our decision and that we would have a meeting of the minds for collaboration. The teachers did not give me any trouble when it was time to have a MD day where whatever had to happen was my decision because they were so rare. I am also intentional about following up via email with bullet points to ensure that everyone knows the game plan and I create parking lots for questions/concerns.

5. *Visit what we Value* – As administrators, we must be aware that integrity is what you do when you think no one is watching. You must conduct yourself as the number one advocate for the school and student success. We must be highly visible and be everywhere. School safety is of utmost importance. We should be conducting walk-throughs; looking at data and helping teachers decide what to do with the data. We must do what we say we are going to do and work hard to implement everything with fidelity. We must be intentional about having crucial conversations when necessary and also be intentional about providing genuine affirmations to our staff and students.

In the book *School Culture Rewired*, Steve Gruenert and Todd Whitaker (2015) explains the difference in school climate and school culture as the climate represents the weather today and school culture represents the weather over a long period of time.

When you are appointed principal, how would you assess the current status of your new school's climate and culture? Identify the characteristics of a school with a positive climate and culture.

When I am appointed principal, I will spend time observing the systems that are already in place to see what works and what does not. I will hold town hall meetings with the students to survey them and collect data from the student body. I also plan to host Muffins with McDonald and Pancakes with the Principal meetings to introduce myself and to hear from the community. I will sit in on department meetings and common planning time to see how teachers interact with each other and after I collect data from multiple sources, I will create a start/stop list. I will work tirelessly to build relational capacity with all stakeholders. I would spend time talking to teachers in groups and individually to get a feel for their wants/need/goals and collaborate with teams to create systems to ensure our success.

A school that has a positive school climate seems more like a home away from home. The teachers work together to achieve maximum student success. They plan together and give common formative assessments. They look at student data and decide how they will use it to impact the learning. They work across grade and content levels to build bridges for students to have cross-curricular learning. They celebrate together, and they share in disappointments together. Teachers take on leadership roles and are trusted to lead the school into new adventures that will create more diverse learning opportunities for our students. We as a staff will work hard and play even harder.

What educational leaders are saying about Natasha McDonald:

"Ms. McDonald is a person of high integrity. She always puts the students first. While working with Ms. McDonald, I always knew she would examine concerns from the point of view of what is best for students."

"Ms. McDonald continuously models servant leadership, ethical decision making, and organizational excellence. She is dedicated to student achievement and school success."

Natasha McDonald's outgoing personality, relational capacity, organization skills, instructional background and relevant administration experience in education makes her a strong candidate for a Campus Principal. She has been a Texas Public Educator for 13 years and has had the distinct honor of working with several phenomenal individuals.

She has had the opportunity to work as a Classroom Teacher, a Literacy Strategist, an Assistant Principal, and an Academic Dean of Instruction. A former principal spent time mentoring her and ultimately inspired her to become an administrator. She is thankful that she has had the opportunity to serve in multiple roles and obtain a wealth of knowledge to share with others.

She has a passion for education, helping others, and has mastered the art of student discipline. She absolutely loves children and understands that we must invest in them as they hold the key to our future. She juggles the roles of wife, mother, mentor, and educator while simultaneously leading teachers in finding ways to analyze student data to get better each day. She finds pleasure in learning new ways to impact student achievement and have challenged herself to address her own personal constraints daily.

As an educator, she is always seeking to better herself and has dedicated herself to a journey of lifelong learning. She is very thankful that she "gets" to be an educator. She understands grit and the growth mindset that is necessary for student success and would love the opportunity to lead scholars as a Campus Principal. The ability to obtain knowledge is a remarkable gift and she puts her heart and soul into learning new things and sharing them with others. With her leadership capabilities, relevant experience, energetic personality, love for kids, and desire to educate, Natasha feels she is a perfect fit to assume the role of principal.

"Do not go where the path may lead, go instead where there is no path and leave a trail." – Ralph Waldo Emerson

Damon M. Qualls

"My mornings begin in my principal's office; we hold hands and pray for the day." – D. Qualls

What motivated or inspired you to become an assistant principal?

I was an only child for twelve years, and during those twelve years, I involved other children in my life by playing school with my cousins. I transformed my bedroom and even my club house into my classroom, where I always led as the teacher. When my "students" began to use the skills I shared with them in their "real school", and were actually successful, I knew that I would be a teacher when I "grew up". This early desire to teach inspired me to seek tutoring opportunities in middle and high school. The joy I found as a tutor in grade school solidified my love for teaching. During my senior year of high school, I learned of a brand new initiative, Call Me MISTER, headquartered at Clemson University, seeking to recruit African American males to become elementary school teachers in the state of South Carolina. Perfect timing! There was no doubt that the path to teaching was one I was called to embark upon.

After eleven successful and rewarding years as a fifth grade teacher, it was time to solidify my influence beyond the walls of my classroom and strive to impact an entire school building. Now in my second year serving as an assistant principal, my daily goal as an administrator is to motivate and encourage the students and staff in my school, as well create and maintain a climate where people desire to be. My mornings begin in my principal's office; we hold hands and pray for the day. We consistently ask for guidance in every situation that will arise and the wisdom to make the best decision. I strive to purposely create an atmosphere and build a culture in which our entire school feels appreciated and achievements, big or small, are celebrated. I have a passion for people, which leads me to quickly recognize the strengths and talents of those around me and effectively collaborate with them to generate superior results in a variety of settings. As an assistant principal, this quality permits me to discover the gifts of individual teachers, as well as students, in an effort to unlock their potential in ways that develop strong leadership skills that lead to academic successes. I commit to do this by affirming the work that each person in our building is doing by speaking words of affirmation, providing the necessary resources, and offering intentional support for effective instructional practices.

What experiences have you had as an assistant principal in each of the seven core areas identified?

Instructional Levers

Data-driven instruction – Like every effective administrator, data drives and determines everything that we do. My greatest accomplishment using data to drive instruction actually took place when I was a teacher leader and continues to have a profound impact on my service as a school administrator. While teaching, I had an opportunity to review state test scores with my principal. We were alarmed at the discrepancy in reading scores between our male and female students, particularly our African-American students. This realization birthed the Men Who Read Program.

The mission and vision of this unique program is geared to bridge the gap between male and female students' standardized test scores in Reading and English Language Arts. We began to expose our young men to professional men in the community like judges, coaches, college athletes, pastors and so many other influential community leaders that enjoy reading and the role it has in their career. Monthly, our gentlemen meet and listen to a guest reader(s) share a book of their choice and discuss how reading has impacted their life.

In 2013, the program added the "Dress for Success" component. We've all heard the phrase, "Dress for Success." What exactly does this mean? This is exactly what the young men wanted to know as well. The program explains confidence consumes us when we "dress up." Imagine how this feeling motivates fourth and fifth graders when all of them are able to wear a blazer for Men Who Read Program days and other important school festivities!

Thanks to several grants from DonorsChoose.org, each participating young men wears a Ralph Lauren, navy blue blazer and a blue and gold tie! With every "Men Who Read" session that passes; the students are able to see the connection between reading well, being successful and looking the part. As I moved into administration, the need was present at my new school, and since implementing the program; it has ignited our participants with a newfound passion for reading.

Observation and feedback – It is so important for administrators to have positive relationships established with their teachers, so when they enter the classroom to observe and provide feedback, the teacher does not feel threatened or intimidated and can continue to facilitate learning, as if the administrator were not in the room. Particularly for emerging teachers, I purposely celebrate their strengths school wide and throughout the community. With teacher shortages becoming prevalent, providing as much positive feedback is a necessity to insure we as administrators develop and maintain quality educators, who are committed to the students and the profession, despite the challenges they encounter. My desire is not to be one of those challenges.

Instructional Planning – Teachers will often come to me asking advice on how to make their lesson plans more creative, allowing for more effective teaching practices. Most recently, I helped a seventh grade math teacher develop a plan for teaching geometry concepts. Together we built a lesson based on music and rap to increase student buy-in. Another example of performing instructional planning would be bringing Social Studies to life with our Rosie the Riveter Day. On this day, my seventh grade female students and teachers dressed up as Rosie the Riveter as they were studying World War II at the time. We celebrated the determined women who stepped into leadership roles to keep The Home Front afloat while men served at war. Finally, I assist my teachers in securing funding for class field trips to witness current Social Studies concepts in real life, such as trips to go see the movie "He Named Me Malala" and excursions to the Biltmore Estate to deepen their understanding of the Industrial Revolution.

Professional Development – As an administrator in a Title 1 school, we are very fortunate to receive state funding that allows us to be creative with our professional development offerings. From sending our teachers and staff to local and state professional development opportunities, to having the funds to provide instruction on the latest technology advancements in education, we are excited about promoting best practices in education. When teachers attend professional development conferences, they return to campus with new and vital information to share with their teams, teaching each other and pushing each other towards excellence.

Cultural Levers

Student culture – In my experience, I have served schools where I've made it my personal mission to create an environment and an atmosphere where not only teachers and staff, but also students can take pride in their school. Celebrated people celebrate people. School spirit and pride, mascots, school-wide celebrations weave together to create a sense of ownership within our faculty and student body. Looking for opportunities for students and teachers to experience success allows me to serve as a catalyst for systemic change. One example of such an endeavor would be recruiting and preparing a group of students to compete in a local Black History Month Trivia Bowl. By bringing back a win for our school, we could ignite an excitement for and pride in our achievements as a school.

In Ken Blanchard's book, *The Servant Leader,* he shares in the beginning pages a quote by Victor Hugo that epitomizes my career as an educator thus far. Hugo states, "Nothing is more powerful than an idea whose time has come." What about transforming the media center into barber shop, inviting master barbers and stylists to teach male students about first impressions, personal hygiene, looking the part and ultimately getting haircuts for the new year, all there in the heart of the media center? What about transforming the library into a five-star restaurant and provide members of the Men Who Read, Dress for Success program a five course meal, in an effort to allow them to apply their newly learned formal dining skills? Forget the fact that the school is 100% poverty, what if we provided Ralph Lauren blazers and neckties in our school colors to every young man in third, fourth and fifth grade, to allow young men to experience personal dress. Ideas, whose time has come, because of the vision of a leader who truly believes that anything is possible.

Staff culture– I chose my current school because I felt I could bring my professional strengths and creative instincts to create a culture for positive change. By working to bridge the business and community partnerships and aligning them with our school's mission and vision, I secured numerous relationships that pushed our internal and external collaboration to the next level. Walking into the building as a first year assistant principal, I knew the importance of building rapport with my faculty. By working alongside them and fostering an environment for positive change and encouragement, I have not only built solid relationships and gained the trust of my faculty, but I have also cultivated a vision for our school that has been embraced by the entire community. Because of the financial challenges many of the families we serve face , teachers don't often receive gifts or tokens of appreciation. During my practicum experience of my administration degree, my principal gave me the responsibility of coordinating American Education Week.

Since that experience, I have made it my goal to celebrate each teacher during American Education week annually. By recruiting business and community partners to donate over $4,500 in prizes and giveaways, I present dozens of prizes to teachers every day of the week. I plan spirit days for every day of the week during which teachers and staff dress up in a variety of costumes. Those faculty and staff members who participate by dressing up email me with the catch phrase, "In It To Win It", in order to qualify for the daily drawing. Prizes range in monetary value from free milkshakes to a free weekend at a local 5-star hotel. By celebrating my teachers and helping make each school day new and exciting, I am cultivating a sense of pride and community within our school building. This same passion to "make ideas happen" keeps my mission as an assistant principal to be so much more than books, behavior, and buses. Our students, teachers and faculty members deserve more.

Managing school leadership teams – One of the first initiatives I began at my current school began with the idea of giving each teacher and staff member a voice in school-wide decisions. By creating a Faculty Council, my teachers meet as individual teams and then choose a representative to attend monthly meetings. This opportunity allows information to be dispersed in an efficient manner and provides a way for each teacher to take part in telling our story, redefining who we are as a school body. As a member of this valuable team, I facilitate each session, create agendas, email reminders and event dates, promote communication within our group, and actively listen to concerns and suggestions.

To provide an accurate reflection of a student's overall learning, our district introduced a grading floor policy for middle and high schools, to begin during the 2016–2017 school year. The policy states a 61 will become the lowest grade a student can receive for an assignment, test or project. Schools were given the opportunity to determine how student assignments would be graded, to ensure students who made below a 61, had a chance to resubmit for a better grade. As the developer and lead of the school's faculty council, I took the lead in orchestrating our school's grading policy. There was expected resistance by some who believed we were "giving students grades" and rewarding undesired behavior. As the leader, I actively listened to all concerns, and collectively we shaped a plan tailored to the needs of our student population.

Using guidelines provided by the district, the faculty council collaborated to develop a policy that worked best for the needs of our student population. The 2015–2016 school year served as an experimental year. Our faculty council took several months to develop our plan and used the last quarter to implement the policy. During this time, I shared quotes and justification from the district as to why we were moving to a grading floor on all of our social media websites and included them in our *Week at a Glance* publication for faculty and staff.

At the conclusion of the third quarter, the faculty council presented our plan to the staff at a faculty meeting. Our presentation was the final product of a collective effort from all stakeholders. Each faculty council member was given a particular part of the plan to present. The presentation was well received because the team had considered every possible point of concern. Leading with a proactive mindset, the team was well prepared to discuss the possibility of assignments being given that lack rigor, to ensure students "master" or pass so select teachers will not have to reteach or adhere to plan in place as stated in policy or an inaccurate reflection of student mastery.

This policy is now in full swing; with complete buy-in from all stakeholders. We continue to demonstrate the policy's relevance by providing consistent opportunities from stakeholders to provide feedback in terms of how the policy is working, by celebrating and sharing accomplishments of the implemented policy and clearly communicating the district's mission and vision as it relates to the policy with all stakeholders. Working together, we can create a culture of positivity and serve as catalysts for productive change within our school.

What specific experiences in your tenure as an assistant principal have allowed you to increase your readiness to assume the role of principal?

Assuming the role of principal takes enormous preparation. During my graduate program, we were highly encouraged by our professors to begin to think, act and respond to situations as a principal. This change in mindset is essential and allows future administrators to have a more holistic view of day-to-day school management and operations.

In addition to solid training through graduate classes and practicums during graduate school, this year I was selected into my district's Assistant Principal's Institute, which was no easy feat.

The process begins with a recommendation from your principal. From the recommendations, candidates are screened and the next level is a district interview with all assistant superintendents and the director of Evaluation and Development.

On average, fifteen candidates are then selected to participate in a year-long study, earning more than twenty hours of professional development.

Monthly, participants are exposed to online dialogues, multiple book studies and highly engaging conversations, with constant observation and feedback from the four assistant superintendents.

Each month has a theme centered on topics that effective principals must have a strong, working knowledge of to be successful, to include instructional leadership, operational management, finance, communication, student achievement and so much more.

Having had this great opportunity afforded to me has given me the chance to build relationships with not only the assistant superintendents, but also the "best of the best" in terms of district principals, who are featured speakers during the meetings. Our sessions also provide real-world application, with "what would you do" skits, placing us in on the spot scenarios and we're forced to respond and make on the spot decisions, sometimes in the midst of difficult conversations.

During the institute, each participant is tasked with identifying an area that they would like to grow in, and then develop a professional goal, with the same requirements and expectations of district principals. Because so much of my previous experience in terms of school finance has been centered around obtaining grants and resources from business partners, I wanted a more solid foundation in school budgets. As a result, with the guidance of my assistant superintendents, I developed a list of strategies and activities that would help me reach my goal, determined how progress would be measured, who I would be accountable to and lastly how I would reward myself when the goal is achieved. Possible obstacles were also determined that might hinder or slow down the process, as well benefits of ultimately obtaining the goal. These types of efforts that place me in real-world situations, where I can think, respond and reflect certainly are beneficial in my journey to principalship.

Choose one of the five practices and explain how you currently demonstrate that practice.

Enable Others to Act

I believe the 21st Century school educator has to possess skills to create and build a brand for their classrooms and schools. With so many incredible school choices for students and parents, a distinct difference has to be made for your school that sets it apart from any other. This holds true to you as an assistant principal. My experiences have allowed me to accomplish this goal.

As a teacher in one of the smallest schools in the largest district in the state of South Carolina, where 100% of students receive free or reduced lunch, what could possibly attract positive attention to our campus?

I utilized our insufficiencies to create opportunities to seek funding to transform our campus one project at a time. In less than four years, with over 127 fully funded grants using DonorsChoose.org, I led our school to over $200,000 in resources to improve every aspect of our day-to-day operation. I could not keep this a secret and began to present our efforts in the district and conferences across the state. In May of 2015, our efforts were recognized in New York City by The Late Show host and DonorsChoose.org Board Member, Stephen Colbert, when he gave me the shock of my career and flash funded every teacher request from South Carolina, totaling over $800,000. Vision is inevitable to have for your school, but it requires financial support.

That next month I was offered a position as an assistant principal. I was absolutely ecstatic; however, I knew that I would no longer be able to write grants through Donors Choose, an organization that I had grown to love. There was no way I could just stop, since the students at the school I was moving to face the same financial challenges.

Now, as an assistant principal, I am able to assist teachers weekly in submitting proposals of their wildest teacher dreams and in less than two years, over $50,000 has been earned to bring "out of the box" endeavors to improve our students' learning experiences. One that we are most proud of is raising over $5,000, an idea I referred to as Mural Mania, transformed bare walls in high traffic areas in that school, with bright, inspiring images, that will foster an engaging, environment for many years to come.

What activities and learning experiences do you recommend for assistant principals aspiring to assume the role of principal?

Activities and Learning Experiences

As an assistant principal, the most primary way to strengthen professional skills in the field of school leadership and administration would be to develop a dynamic relationship with your current building principal. As early as my initial interview, my connection with my principal was evident. Her beliefs and my beliefs were aligned, and I sincerely felt I would grow under her guidance and leadership. I started building a solid, trusting relationship with my school leader. Right away we started the habit of praying with one another before the school day began and consulting and collaborating with each other throughout the day. In my opinion, if you do not have a positive working relationship with your principal, you need to find another building. Who better to help guide you in the right direction and serve as your biggest cheerleader than your principal? Another suggestion I have would be to get involved with a district program of study for assistant principals that address the foundational truths of leadership and the key tenets of quality professional growth. In my program, we focus on instructional leadership, operational management, financial literacy, communication, and student achievement through classes, online dialogues, book studies, and small group discussions. This type of program is vital for any professional in education who wants to take leadership to the next level.

What do you believe are five key characteristics of effective leadership? Describe how you demonstrate each of those characteristics.

Five (5) key characteristics of effective leadership

Innovation – Effective leaders should know how to combine a variety of leadership styles to develop a creative way to lead, guide, and direct a program. As creative visionaries, innovative leaders brainstorm big ideas and motivate people around them to help turn those dreams into realities. Part of my role as an innovative leader is to make each day new and exciting, celebrating the hard work and accomplishments of school faculty and students, and recognizing the visions of other faculty members. By using a powerful imagination and effective communication skills, I strive to communicate a clear vision, generate motivation, and foster enthusiasm.

Flexibility –Flexibility is a key tenet of leadership as it is crucial to understand that people have needs and things may not always go as planned. Life happens: things come up; personnel issues arise. People are people—that's just part of being human. By remembering that you can't grip your plans too tightly prevents each snag from resulting in disaster. Go with the flow, stay excited, and keep it moving.

Approachability – In leadership, you want to build relationships with your colleagues in order to build rapport and trust with your team. I am the type of leader who plans faculty outings, celebrates my teachers' birthdays with strobe lights, music and food, throws parties when one of my colleagues accomplishes something exciting, and always keeps my door open and office inviting. Teachers are not intimidated by me because they see me as a colleague, a leader and not a "boss."

Humility – As a servant leader, humility is a key concept in working as a professional. One aspect of humility is pursuing continuous learning opportunities to stay relevant with the newest developments in educational best practices. Last summer I was selected and attended a professional education program at Harvard University titled "Improving Schools: The Art of Leadership." Participating in this program strengthened my leadership skills, efficacy, and ability to support teacher development and student achievement. After intense collaboration with over 150 principals from literally across the globe, the tools I returned back with allowed me to practice exploring various methods for addressing leadership challenges and improved my ability to lead and manage my current school. In addition to this trip of a lifetime to Harvard, I was also named to the South Carolina ASCD (Association for Supervision and Curriculum Development) Emerging Leader program, for always seeking innovative ways to continue my path as a lifetime learner and creating an environment to develop and the support the "whole child."

Confidence – One part of effective leadership that I am passionate about is demonstrating a sense of confidence in everything I do. Every day I seek to share the mission and vision of my school. By talking to business partners to acquire resources and meeting with parents about new ideas and concerns, I am building a community to serve as a unified body of stakeholders to keep our successes and accomplishments growing. Confident leaders are knowledgeable about what they are communicating and can articulate what they are saying in a clear and understandable way. Having confidence in sharing new information, presenting data, or describing a newly implemented plan will help teachers and staff trust what you are saying and increase buy-in. If teachers do not sense confidence, they will not believe what you have to say.

When you are appointed principal, how would you assess the current status of your new school's climate and culture? Identify the characteristics of a school with a positive climate and culture.

Climate vs. Culture

As a newly appointed principal, I would assess the school's climate by immediately evaluating the front office greeting. As soon as you arrive to a school campus, one can quickly identify whether or not the school is a place where both adults and students want to be. Simply walking down the halls and witnessing interactions between students and teachers will speak volumes. Observing teachers at their duty posts to see how excited staff members are when performing their "extra tasks", or checking to see if passersby pick up a candy wrapper off of the floor, or even observing bulletin boards and wall art; is it current, is it rigorous? I am a firm believer that schools with a healthy and progressive climate post relevant and recent student work. There are photographs visible of all stakeholders engaged in activities that support the mission and the vision of the school.

Overall, I look too see how teachers and students take pride in their school. I would evaluate the culture of my new school by scheduling one-on-one meetings with everyone in the building, from the plant engineer, cafeteria staff, secretaries to teachers, giving ample time to complete these interviews before the first day of school. These meetings would allow me to get to know each person in the building, learn about recent school trends, and listen to staff concerns. Sometimes first year principals arrive in a school that is not "broken" and make the mistake of trying to change systems that have a proven track record. This will not be my testimony.

My wife, a first year principal, always says, "Slow is fast." These informative sessions would allow me to learn the simple things, but important things. For example, how long they've been working at the school, what they've noticed during their career at the school, any shift in student demographics, how long teachers normally stay at the school, etc. I would also study social media posts, if available, and look at posts and responses from parents and community members to analyze how many on- and off-campus positive school stakeholders' relationships the school has established. Creating a strong social media presence as an assistant principal, has not only been beneficial in terms of developing a school brand, but it also allows me to learn the community, family connections and ultimately the pulse the school's reputation.

What educational leaders are saying about Damon Qualls:

"Damon attacks every task with a gusto seldom seen. His enthusiasm is infectious and has spread throughout the building. I cannot say enough good things about Damon Qualls!"

– Robin B. Mill, Principal-Current Supervisor

Currently serving as an assistant principal at a middle school in Greenville, South Carolina, Damon Qualls cultivates his gift of leadership and service through continuing education, invaluable experiences, and professional collaboration.

His passion for education began when he was just a youngster "playing school". The Call Me MISTER Program served as a catalyst for his career, allowing him to travel the nation for speaking engagements with community organizations, school districts, and political leaders, sharing the need of a more diverse teacher workforce, specifically in South Carolina elementary schools. The MISTER initiative provided Damon life-changing opportunities, including being featured on the nationally syndicated Oprah Winfrey Show, a feature in JET Magazine, an interview with TIME Magazine, an appointment to the NASA Pre-Service Teacher Conference as an Ambassador from the state of South Carolina, and featured documentaries for ABC News of New York and SCeTV of Columbia, SC.

Damon graduated from Benedict College in 2004 with a Bachelor's in Elementary Education and Columbia College in 2006, where he earned a Master of Education degree in Divergent Learning. He earned a second Master's degree from Southern Wesleyan University in School Leadership and Administration in December of 2013.

As a classroom teacher for 11 years in a Title One school, Damon's students faced many challenges. He shared with them the realization that education is the vehicle to drive them towards a more promising future. His goal is to provide students a temporary escape from their pressing worries through the joys of meaningful experiences and exposure to what life has to offer. Damon is using this platform to train teachers across the state on how he obtains credible results from a student population that is stereotypically at-risk or unproductive.

To ensure his students had an equal opportunity to be academically triumphant despite major budget cuts, Damon to date has acquired through grants, over $200,000 for his school(s) and $65,000 for his own classroom.

In May of 2015 Damon represented over a quarter million teachers at the DonorsChoose.org National Partner Summit, where he shared his journey with Donors Choose. Much to his surprise, he was joined on the last day of the summit by comedian and nationally syndicated talk show host Stephen Colbert, with an announcement that $800,000 would be directed to the public schools of South Carolina. This announcement was covered by every major news and social media outlet. As a result, Damon interviewed with MSNBC, PoliticsNation with Al Sharpton, CBS, Robyn Young, and National Public Radio/NPR.

Damon has implemented mentor programs, such as the Men Who Read Program, that have been duplicated across the country. Damon enjoys presenting on the local, state and national levels, empowering fellow educators to seek opportunities to improve their classroom, school, and local community.

Damon finds great joy in working as an assistant principal and looks forward to continuing his pursuit to change the world, one student at a time.

"The secret to success is good leadership, and good leadership is all about making the lives of your team members or workers better." – Tony Dungy

Dr. Najla Solomon

"The efforts of a turnaround leader, must be more drastic, deliberate and at times must incite calculated risks." – N. Solomon

What motivated or inspired you to become an Assistant Principal?

The motivation/inspiration to become a public school assistant principal came from a spiritual and self-preservation calling. This decision was centered on the premise of following a "call to action" that was placed on me by others who were either in the profession previously, those currently as well as others who were inclined at some point in my educational journey to discuss with me the direction in which they foresaw my career shaping. Moreover, my response to answer this plight was the compelling sense to become integral in changing the paradigm shift of practitioners, becoming responsible for dissipating the generational curses that plague African-American and other minority neighborhoods while becoming accountable for increasing not only the educational awareness of urban children; also, wanting to shape and nurture their social and emotional needs.

The desire to be able to impact a child's educational perspectives as an administrator from a larger scale as opposed to a smaller group of children confined to only my assigned classroom as a teacher provided greater opportunities and chances for me to be a "change agent."

Bambrick-Santoyo (2012) in *Leverage Leadership* identifies seven core areas of school leadership, which are referred to as levers. What experiences have you had as an assistant principal in each of the seven core areas identified?

As an assistant principal of a priority school in the State of New Jersey, I have been very fortunate to lead change within each of the elements as specified by Bambrick-Santoyo. A priority school in New Jersey is defined as being among the lowest-performing five percent of Title I schools. As a priority school administrator, my leadership ability is gauged by how effectively I institute what the New Jersey Department of Education (NJDOE) defines as the 8 Turn Around Principles under the supervision of the Regional Achievement Center (RAC). These eight principles are centered on the essentials of the author. They are school leadership, school climate/culture, effective instruction, curriculum/assessment/and intervention system, effective staffing practices, enabling the effective use of data, effective use of time and effective family and community engagement. These elements much like Bambrick-Santoyo are utilized to measure my performance practices on a quarterly basis throughout each academic school year. Each decision that is made is designed around data based outcomes. These outcomes are taken from sources such as but not limited to: survey data, academic performance, attendance rates, behavior data and observation and walkthrough outcomes.

Prior to determining next steps for any school-based decision smart goals are developed at the start of the year through a plan called the School Improvement Plan (SIP). The SIP is drafted based on the outcomes from any of the aforementioned data sources and based on outcomes from the State's Quality School Review (QSR). There are a total of four overarching Smart Goals and four interim goals for each developed Smart Goal with the assistance of the School Improvement Panel (ScIP). This panel is comprised at the start of each school year made up of teachers, administrators and other support staff. These Smart and interim goals developed are centered on areas of curriculum/instruction and culture/climate. For each goal developed there are six to ten action steps that are designed to assist with goal implementation. Interim goals are developed to assist with determining progress and outcomes that inform the committee of next steps, alignment of action steps to goals, factors to consider, and any adjustments that may be needed throughout the course of the year as determined by data review and reflection. Observations and walkthroughs are conducted on a frequent basis to better understand what is needed to foster teacher capacity, professional development needs and how does the development of the plan directly impact student progress. Professional Learning Communities (PLC) and Vertical Articulation teams meet on a regular basis to ensure that effective instructional planning, assessment design, and strategy based instruction are utilized uniformly from content to content.

These areas of school improvement are analyzed on a frequent basis by building administrators, RAC, school-based supervisors, district personnel, teachers as well as school improvement teams.

What specific experiences in your tenure as an assistant principal have allowed you to increase your readiness to assume the role of principal?

The experiences within my tenure as an assistant principal that have increased my readiness to assume the role of principal have been many. I have been fortunate enough to learn and/or be part of learning environments from Pre-K-12. These environments have provided a sound understanding of curriculum and instructional practices therein, widened my understanding of content standards, as well as fostered insight of how primary, intermediate, middle school and high school students learn best. The opportunities I had in curriculum writing, serving as professional development facilitator, participation on steering committees, testing coordination and a litany of others opportunities have allowed me to have a diverse portfolio and background on understanding sound curriculum and instructional practices.

Moreover, I have had the opportunity to be part of two priority schools in New Jersey with both moving from the bottom of priority status to performing at a much higher standard than where progress was initially indicated as determined by the State. Specifically, each year the current priority school I am at has made demonstrated significant increase in its overall student growth percentiles within the past three years.

We were recently recognized by the NJDOE and RAC for exceptional student academic growth on the State's Partnership for Assessment of Readiness for College and Careers (PARCC) assessment. This growth has occurred both in literacy and math. Entering into the role of principal requires someone who is an instructional leader. Having an understanding of the role of an instructional leader and performing as such in the role of the assistant principal has equally prepared me to enter into the role of principal.

In the book *Leadership Challenge,* Kouzes and Posner (2002) identify "Five Practices of Exemplary Leadership". Choose one of the five practices and explain how you currently demonstrate that practice.

In leadership, today, it is important to not stick to the status quo. Kouzes and Posner (2002) talk about **Challenging the Process.** As a priority school administrator, I am faced with challenges daily. Being a turnaround leader is very different than being a leader who wants to sustain school improvement. The efforts of a turnaround leader must be more drastic, deliberate and at times must incite calculated risks. In my current school, we have a growing number of English Language Learners (ELL) thus; we must find a myriad of methods to support the academic and social progress of this sub-group. Our district does not have a newcomer's program therefore; we have had to find innovative approaches to meet their very diverse needs. The district's model bilingual program is to have students exposed to a dual language program where students receive instruction one week in native language and the alternating week in English. Unfortunately, the data showed that our students were not becoming fluent in English or exiting the bilingual program as rapidly as students in other surrounding districts. Therefore, the NJDOE/ RAC challenged us to plan for the upcoming year by finding an innovative method to meet their academic needs and supporting their learning of the English Language.

Over the summer, we began to put plans together to restructure our program internally and work with the State to accomplish this task. Rather than have students exposed to native language and English on alternating weeks, the decision was made to restructure our master schedule so that we could implement a part-time bilingual instructional model. This model would allow our children to become completely emerged in the English Language through the core content in Math, ELA, and Elective courses with ESL teacher support (for first second year ELL students) and have them receive instruction in their native language in science and social studies only. This was a bold move because they would spend more than 70% of their school day emerged in English based instruction and the other 30% in their native language. This plan was structured to counter attack the low passing rates students received on their ACCESS for ELLs Language Proficiency assessment as well as being able to take the State PARCC assessment in English with specified content and language acquisition. In order to successfully accomplish this, the district had to submit a waiver to the NJDOE to get their final approval to deviate from the already established district model.

Talk about challenging the status quo! This was not heard of in our district and to want to deviate to try to do something different and apart from others; we were faced with the initial thoughts of what if we fail, to how will our staff receive this, and putting into perspectives the thoughts of the community and parental support. Prior to the inception of this concept we spent countless hours meeting with stakeholders, notifying parents and teachers, discussions on data, the projected plan of action and anticipated outcomes or foreseen successes. This action was put into place at the start of the year; however, we were on a roll for the first three to four months of school until we were faced with a minor setback. This setback resulted in us having to reorganize our thinking and restructure scheduling. While our initial plan had been abandoned, we began to see those scholars who were part of the part-time model show improvement in their overall cycle grades in both math and literacy. Needless to say, the original concept we planned had extreme potential for the scholars involved.

What activities and learning experiences do you recommend for assistant principals aspiring to assume the role of principal?

Any assistant principals who have a growing desire to assume the role of principal should become part of a leadership consortium and become active in that consortium, position themselves around a principal or other leaders whether current or former who have been recognized as an effective instructional leader, learn what they know, build a network of support, become familiar with effective leadership practices, understand the hearts, motivations and desires of teachers and students, be prepared to learn more than you ever had in the past, read and research more than you ever thought you would, and always be ready to and prepared to still teach when necessary. As an instructional leader, you will always have to and look towards understanding how to be reflective in your practices as an administrator so that you can continue to grow and develop as an instructional leader.

What do you believe are five (5) key characteristics of effective leadership? Describe how you demonstrate each of those characteristics.

It is my belief that the following are five of the most powerful characteristics of effective leadership: **Become partners with your constituents, lead by example, be inspirational** (find the hidden potential of the persons you lead), **foster teacher growth and opportunity** and **become an architect.**

It is important for any effective leader to work with constituents to plan, develop and structure how best to improve the quality of a child's educational performance. This means that he/she must be able to establish a vision/mission as well as work with constituents on how to best facilitate and sustain it. At the start of my current role, we met with our staff over the summer and the start of the school year to share with them the current state of the school, the impositions placed on us by the NJDOE, data mined to support the status of school, interviewed staff and utilized data outcomes from these sessions to begin to establish school based teams, action planning and goal setting with appropriate personnel. This effort was made to inform staff, review elements of our vision and mission of the school, the direction the administrative team wanted to take the school, and for staff to have equal buy-in and be supportive of the revised process.

Throughout the process of being an instructional leader, I have found it better to demonstrate for my constituents my expectations. For example, in the past, I have had expectations of my staff to utilize an instructional practice, if it is important for me to tell them about the practice, then it is equally important for me to show them how to implement this practice. In previous years, there were many occasions after a PLC, vertical articulation or professional development session, that I have gone into classrooms and work with teachers to demonstrate for them how to implement recommended or directed practices. When this was initially done, students as well as teachers were amazed because either they have never been led by an administrator who came into the classroom to work collaboratively with them to teach or he only time they have seen an administrator in the classroom was for evaluation purposes or simple visitations. This type of leadership has allowed staff to see and know that the art of teaching is still apparent to building level administrators and the level of respect that my staff had for me increased tremendously; especially, coming into a situation where I was an outsider. There had to be some level of trust that needed to be built and established between myself and my new staff and this I believe is what began to bridge that gap.

Being inspirational and fostering growth and opportunity are supportive characteristics. These two go hand in hand, because it is important for an effective leader to tap into the hidden potential of their teachers and provide opportunities for them to develop that gift. These two are so important especially in a priority school where many teachers become downtrodden, burned out, and often will choose to leave the profession.

At the start of my first year in my current school I noticed that I had an English Language Arts (ELA) teacher who would clam up each time I walked into her classroom to observe her. I noticed that this teacher, while some of her evaluations did not always reflect her effectiveness, had hidden potential that she was fearful to release. Our post-conferences would at times be filled with her saying that she could not do what I needed her to do or often be filled with questions about why, how, when and self doubt. By the third walk-through conducted on her and our meeting thereafter, I decided to change the tone of conversation with her. The newer conversations began with yes you can, I know you can, and we will work together to ensure that you are successful. There was even one conversation where I told her that she would become one of my master ELA teachers in the very near future. She still doubted herself after that conversation. Rather than spend time on citing the negative, I told her what I expected of her, how she was more than capable and elicited from her what she needed from me to become the master teacher I knew she could become. After those initial meetings, she began to take me at my word, she would show up to my office as frequently as she could with her notebook to document all that she could to learn what I knew about effective ELA instruction. We began to have instructional conversations centered on research, implementation and outcomes. I began directing her toward continued support externally and internally and began providing non-evaluative observations to see how she began to implement what she learned. Each year her Student Growth Percentiles (SGP) improved from year one to year two by 7 points and year two to year three over 13 points. She was awarded the State's Teacher of Year in year two and by year three she became rated by the NJDOE as highly effective for an increased SGP. In order for her to obtain what she did, she had open her mind to an understanding that she held the capacity to perform at a greater aptitude as an educator. Inspiring and building are two very integral components to being an effective instructional leader.

Lastly, becoming an architect is part of how an effective leader provides his/her constituents with the plans on how school improvement will take place and can work with staff to develop a road map toward this type of work. The previous school year, the SIP team decided that it would be appropriate to begin doing work centered on the improvement of discipline in the school as the end of year data determined there was an immediate need. The team put together within the SIP Smart Goals, interim goals, action steps, and resources to support this process. As the assistant principal, I was assigned the role of facilitating the design of this plan for supporting culture and climate and working directly with SIP members to design an effective plan that would meet the approval of the RAC and district. By the summer of the preceding school year the SIP was approved by State and district personnel. Now part of my role this year is to work directly with Positive Behavior Support in Schools through Rutger's University to bring the designed plan into fruition for the upcoming school year. An effective leader must work collaboratively with teams, institutions and other leaders to be the architect of a plan that would positively impact current student performance in all areas of school improvement. When we participated in our initial RAC review and had to report out on the effectiveness of our goal that was in support of discipline; we could report a decrease in office conduct referrals and suspensions.

In the book *School Culture Rewired*, Steve Gruenert and Todd Whitaker (2015) explains the difference in school climate and school culture as the climate represents the weather today and school culture represents the weather over a long period of time.

When you are appointed principal, how would you assess the current status of your new school's climate and culture? Identify the characteristics of a school with a positive climate and culture.

It is my belief that an effective way to obtain a pulse or the heartbeat of any school (culture) is to look at survey data that is centered on assessing aspects of school culture, interview staff individually, look at past observation data and feedback, interview students/parents and collect survey data accordingly as well, meet with current Parent Teacher Organization (PTO) and ascertain data collection that deals with absenteeism rates, academic performance, and discipline data. These data points are connected to determining the culture of a building.

The characteristics of a school with a positive climate and culture include the following: students obtaining academic successes (learning environment), productivity of leaders, teachers, and support personnel (staff who are willing to work above and beyond contractual obligations), cleanliness of physical environment and a positive social/emotional environment.

What educational leaders are saying about Dr. Najla Solomon

"Mrs. Solomon represents herself as a professional at all times in an extremely professional manner. I am truly impressed by her commitment to excellence. She represents an uncompromising effort to promote quality education for all students and never loses sight of their needs in all she does."

"Dr. Solomon is a natural leader who rarely needs supervision. She brings a high a level professionalism to her work and she exudes positive energy, confidence, and a determination to do the very best she can in any given situation."

Dr. Najla Solomon is a first-generation college graduate. While attending college, she received the confirmation from a professor who strongly encouraged her to major in English Literature and minor in Secondary Education. By 2000, Najla obtained her Bachelor's degree from St. Peter's College in Jersey City, NJ, directly after she returned to St. Peter's to work toward obtaining a Master's degree in Supervision and Urban Leadership (graduated 2002). She recently earned her Doctorate in Education for School Leadership from Kean University in 2015.

Dr. Solomon has served as an educator for 17 years. Six of those years were spent as a teacher of English Literature and Language Arts, three years as a Literacy Coach and eight years spent as an administrator. Her experiences range from Pre-K to 12th grade. Early in her career, she had the pleasure of working in her hometown of East Orange (returning to her city as a teacher in the middle school from which she graduated), larger districts such as Newark, Paterson, and Jersey City. Two years of her administrative journey were spent in a newly founded charter high school, three years as a K-8 vice principal and her current role is a middle school vice principal in the city of Plainfield for the past three years. These combined experiences have allowed Dr. Solomon to gain further insight into the organizational structures of private, charter and public sectors of education.

Her current role as vice principal requires her to lead the "Turnaround" effort at the middle school level for what the New Jersey Department of Education classifies as a Priority School. As a priority school administrator, she has been charged with increasing the overall academic achievement, college readiness, attendance/behavioral rates as well as make improvements in the overall culture/climate of the school. This effort is a challenging endeavor, however, Dr. Solomon believes the reward of improving the learning environment for children is the reason why she entered into the field of education. She and the administrative team in her current school, were recognized by the Acting Commissioner of Education and the Regional Achievement Center (RAC) from the New Jersey Department of Education as making significant improvement in student academic growth over the past three years.

She is an active member of Black Parents of Successful Sons Empowered (B.P.O.S.S.E.) and has spent time in the past coaching recreational basketball for five and six year-old children. Additionally, she is part of a Steering Committee Partnership between Kean University and her district for a teacher mentor federal grant funded program, was a Supplemental Education Provider for the New Jersey Department of Education as well as has served as a facilitator of professional development for concepts on school leadership, curriculum development, Achieve NJ, new teacher training, literacy based concepts, testing and data analysis.

Outside of her professional and personal commitments, she enjoys bike riding, routine exercise, traveling, going to the movies (alone), dining at quaint restaurants and dives, reading and spending quality time with her husband and sons.

"To teach is a calling and no one should enter into this profession foolheartedly. It is not for the weak or faint of heart. It is rather for those who dare to challenge those who otherwise would think that our children are not worth the very item generations before them have fought hard for them to acquire."
— Dr. Najla Solomon

Jessie Williams

"An effective leader is a communicator." – J. Williams

What motivated or inspired you to become an assistant principal?

As a young ambitious man, I always had the desire to advance and excel. I knew that I had more to offer to the profession of education. Being a natural born leader assuming the role of assistant principal fit me perfectly. It allowed me to give more to the field of education and exercise my ability to lead not only students, but adults as well. I enjoy the challenges that come with the position and could not envision myself in any other role outside of being principal or district level administrator at this point in my life.

Bambrick-Santoyo (2012) in Leverage Leadership identifies seven core areas of school leadership, which are referred to as levers. What experiences have you had as an assistant principal in each of the seven core areas identified?

Instructional Levers:

1. *Data Driven instruction:* Every year, we sit down with our data derived from district and state level standardized testing. I use it to inform the decisions we need to make concerning professional development and support for the classroom teachers. We also use this data to help our teachers pinpoint their focus of instruction for each level of student in their classroom.

2. *Observation and Feedback:* I spend at least 20 minutes in a classroom making observations and providing those teachers I have observed solid feedback based on our chosen observation tools. For teachers on formal evaluation, I spend up to 45 minutes in those classrooms not daily, however. I meet with the first year teachers to have open dialogue about my observations in their classroom, making suggestions based on that teacher needs. We then use the formal observations to evaluate those teachers.

3. *Instructional Planning:* Instructional planning is the long range and short range plans for teachers. We expect to see the short range plans when we walking in the classroom. The key components that we look for are the standards being addressed, the objective of the lesson, the activities that support the objective, plans for assessment, and the use of technology. I have found, while in the classroom, that if you plan with the end in mind, you would have planned well.

4. *Professional Development:* I have led professional development sessions for our teachers and staff in the area of differentiated instruction, common

core math standards, using the NWEA learning continuum, PBIS, classroom management, team building, using the fire extinguisher, safe workplace tidbits.

Cultural Levers

1. *Student Culture*: I have developed two signature-mentoring programs for our school, Bow Tie Gents and Girl in Pearls. I also develop the criteria for afterschool clubs and programming. I am the sponsor for the flag patrol as well. I created and designed the positive referrals used to recognize students for exceeding school wide expectations.
2. *Staff Culture*: Along with professional development, I am big on staff development. I have brought in folks from insurance companies to talk about building for their retirement. I have conducted team-building exercises with the entire faculty and staff. I encourage teachers to pursue higher education degrees and take advantage of educational opportunities outside of the PD we provide here.
3. *Managing School Leadership Teams*: I am the crisis team leader, the Total School Cluster Grouping leader, and administrator in charge of the kindergarten, second and fourth grades, and Related Arts Team.

What specific experiences in your tenure as an assistant principal have allowed you to increase your readiness to assume the role of principal?

There are two experiences that have prepared me to assume the role of principal. Those experiences are my role as the team leader for specific school leadership teams as mentioned above and the opportunity to create and manage two signature-mentoring programs. These experiences have helped me to understand the role of principal by allowing me to see what it is like to create and operate a budget within school parameters, become and instructional leader that is responsible for the professional development of groups of teachers, and ensuring I have the backing of the community when I pursue efforts in the school.

In the book Leadership Challenge, Kouzes and Posner (2002) identify "Five Practices of Exemplary Leadership". Choose one of the five practices and explain how you currently demonstrate that practice.

I lean more towards **Challenge the Process**. I tend to analyze the system to see what works and is not working and figure out why something works or why something does not work. I am constantly looking at ways to improve our master schedule to allow for more time spent on instruction and at the same time allow students to have much needed downtime. Every year, I meet with team leaders for the grade levels to get their input on the master schedule, so that I can craft the best schedule. I never rest on this "schedule worked last year, why change it" mentality. I also always try to find ways to ensure that what we do in the classroom is having profound learning impacts on our children, so I spend my time observing and using my observations to share best practices based on these observations of model teachers with the entire teaching staff.

What activities and learning experiences do you recommend for assistant principals aspiring to assume the role of principal?

I encourage participation in any leadership development series offered by your district for new administrators or those who want refreshers. Take advantage of courses and offerings from the state department of education. Attend and participate in conferences for administrators. Spend lots of time doing what most impacts the teaching and learning in your school building.

What do you believe are five (5) key characteristics of effective leadership? Describe how you demonstrate each of those characteristics.

1. An effective leader needs to be a people person. I demonstrate this with my daily positive attitude and my genuine concern for my fellow educators.
2. An effective leader needs to make sure that they are getting personal and professional development. I am currently reading books that elevate my intellect and as well as my soul.
3. An effective leader is a communicator. I am careful with choosing my words and always mindful of what settings I am in when speaking. I strive to ensure that my grammar is correct.
4. An effective leader needs to strive for balance. I only stay after school until 4 p.m. three days a week. Other days, I leave at 4 to be able to get my son. I also find time to have fun. Finally, I take care of my health by eating clean most of the time and working out.

5. An effective leaders needs to take risks sometimes. Changing the master schedule took some challenge, but no major resistance. I was afraid that the folks would want the same schedule and not be open to change

In the book *School Culture Rewired*, Steve Gruenert and Todd Whitaker (2015) explains the difference in school climate and school culture as the climate represents the weather today and school culture represents the weather over a long period of time (overall).

When you are appointed principal, how would you assess the current status of your new school's climate and culture? Identify the characteristics of a school with a positive climate and culture.

I plan to meet with each staff member and also teams during the summer and possibly through the first month of the school to determine what we are doing well and what needs to be improved as a school. These face to face meetings will give me lots information about that staff member as well. I would then meet face to face with parents as much as possible, business partners, and local churches just to hear what they know about our school and to give them updates. This would give me a good gauge on the overall moral of the school and the impressions our school are making. I would use this data to develop appropriate staff development activities.

A school with a positive climate:

1. Happy smiling teachers.
2. Everyone speaks in respectful tones and manners.
3. The parents are very supportive and spend lots of time in our building.
4. Teaching and learning is priority.
5. Students know the positive expectations of the school and are modeling them.

What educational leaders are saying about Jessie Williams:

"Jessie has a passion to help students find success especially students who need the extra support. This priority helps him an effective leader. He also has patience and compassion for his faculty. They know he cares for them."

Jessie Williams is native of Mount Pleasant, South Carolina, and youngest of three children. He is married to the former Wyona Thompson. They have one son Elijah.

In 1993, he graduated from USC-Columbia with a Bachelor of Arts in History. He completed a Master of Arts in Teaching-Elementary Education degree in 1996 and in 2006 a Master of Education degree in Educational Administration all from USC-Columbia.

He started his career in education as a substitute teacher and then as a teaching assistant at a high school in South Carolina. He reorganized the high school's Gospel Choir and sponsored the only fraternity ever organized on that campus. Upon receiving certification, he took his first teaching job at a middle school where he worked for three years. In those three short years, he was able to revive the defunct yearbook staff and co-founded a boys to men mentoring program. He was also runner-up for the prestigious award of teacher of the year. After leaving that middle school, he started teaching at an elementary school teaching third and fifth graders. He taught there for six years. While there he organized a boys' choir. The first ever in the history of that school and was able to secure grant funding to sustain the budget of that group from the state's EIA grant source. He is currently an Assistant Principal, a position he has held since the 2005-06 school year. This is his 22nd year in education. Mr. Williams organized and oversees two mentoring programs called Girls In Pearls and BowTie Gents aimed at sharing important life skills with fifth grade girls and boys. He is also an entrepreneur that works to ensure that equal justice under the law is extended to all people.

He grew up in the church and is an ordained elder in the Church of God In Christ. He also is a Minister of Music. He is also blessed to serve as the Director of the South Carolina Jurisdiction COGIC Scholastic Motivation Ministries. These ministries are designed to help young people exude excellence in academics and in all settings and still maintain being a Christian.

In his free time, he loves attending Carolina football and basketball games, bowling, watching movies, and eating great food with family and friends.

"It must be borne in mind that the tragedy of life doesn't lie in not reaching your goal. The tragedy lies in having no goal to reach." – Benjamin E. Mays

Dr. La Shawn Denise Witt

"I have learned that building a trusting community is key." – L. Witt

What motivated or inspired you to become an assistant principal?

Over the years, a handful of my mentors would continuously approach me about advancing into a leadership position. I really had no interest and was perfectly fine with my four walls and 150 or so students. Over time I began to seek out ways that I could benefit the school and the community through my work. It is here; where I began to take on adjunct responsibilities that were outside the classroom. With all of the outside classroom and admin designee experiences, I decided to pursue an assistant principal position. At this time I felt I was ready for a new chapter in my educational career in helping to lead a school and making a greater impact by providing support to teachers, supporting families and providing support to the children who needed the most help. I was interested because I wanted to have a larger impact upon education and creating an effective and engaging learning environment for students. I wanted to take on a buffer role in the education process, if you will.

As a teacher, I focused mainly on educating my students; making sure they were able to learn on their own. As an assistant principal, I saw an opportunity to work with all students and turn our scholars into citizens. Here I am today, an assistant principal at the secondary level. My goal as an assistant principal is to continually help to create an instructional environment in which all students are able to develop to their optimal ability, both academically and socially emotionally. The most rewarding aspect of being an assistant principal is being able to foster a campus environment where learning is valued and teachers and students alike benefit from a mutually positive relationship. I most look forward to solving issues that arise and that typically prevent either teachers or students from benefiting from the learning experience. Removing obstacles to growth will ensure a school culture conducive to learning for a successful school experience for all.

Bambrick-Santoyo (2012) in *Leverage Leadership* identifies seven core areas of school leadership, which are referred to as levers. What experiences have you had as an assistant principal in each of the seven core areas identified?

I have had many experiences as an assistant principal with both instructional and cultural levels. Part of my duties on the leadership team is to oversee the department chairs in reviewing assessment data and gathering feedback to report out to the larger staff. Assessments are the roadmap to rigor. We can test students all day long, but until we review, analyze and discuss the data we will never know how to drive instruction. As a teacher, I would review my quiz results. If I saw that most of the class missed a concept, I made sure to reteach and retest before I would move on to the next chapter. On a larger scale, it works the same for school-wide data. My conversations with staff are driven by data and we make data driven decisions for driving our instructional strategies.

I try my best to get into the classrooms daily. It is almost impossible on some days. Observations are important for various reasons. Walking into a classroom to observe can often be very stressful for a teacher or sometimes inviting. It just depends on the teacher! Observations allow for conversations with teachers on how they are delivering the content. Observations have allowed me to identify key teachers who I have placed in leadership roles, provided me with opportunities to speak to parents about students and behavior concerns and just an overall support to my teachers.

As a leader you set the foundation for instructional planning. Most of this planning comes out of working with your leadership team after reviewing the data. The importance of meeting with your team is to design objectives and instruct teachers to build around those objectives. Serving as an instructional leader has given me the opportunity to work with teachers to build lessons and utilize instructional strategies that have proven successful with our student population.

After successful review of data and instructional planning, I have had many opportunities to provide and plan professional development trainings for staff. After I have had conversations with my leadership teams and provided feedback to teachers on observations, I have used the summers to plan out trainings that will prove beneficial to my staff. Over the years, instructional leadership has proven that we always have to discover new ways to think about the practice and learn how to design meaningful trainings for the teaching staff.

I have always been passionate about understanding and fostering school culture. I find it valuable to serve as role model for my students and staff. People learn by watching just as they learn by doing. Observing the actions of others influences how they respond to their environment and cope with unfamiliar situations.

What do you want your teachers to say about your leadership? Great staff culture comes from careful development of habits that build a strong staff community. Teachers need to be inspired and motivated. I pride myself on being the cheerleader for the teachers that I work with. I find the higher satisfied they are the more committed to the success of our school they want to be. Teachers need to know the school's core mission and be unified in putting it into place.

I have varied experiences with managing school leadership teams. I have worked with school leadership teams to plan out instructional strategies and work with providing high quality professional development opportunities. In addition, managing these teams has allowed for successful student academic success.

What specific experiences in your tenure as an assistant principal have allowed you to increase your readiness to assume the role of principal?

As an assistant principal, I have always been blessed to work for great principals. Serving in this role has allowed me the opportunity to learn and grow as a school leader. Being an assistant principal is not a sexy job; it's messy, it's real, it's not for the faint at heart. We spend significant energy managing the emotions of adults; we are the front lines of discipline, parent complaints, family crises and frustrated teachers or community members. There is not one assistant principal that I know that will disagree with me.

I have learned that building a trusting community is key. Not everyone will trust you, but I learned through experiences that building a culture that values the school community above all else has been what's more important. Trust will eventually come.

You are going to hear a lot of complaints from everyone as an administrator, some valid, many not, but you have to validate and listen to ALL. I learned from experience that validating without emotions is the best approach. It is something that I am still working on today, but it is very important. Validate those problems and help the person with the problem find ways to solve it, rather than doing all the work yourself.

I can't overestimate the importance of data. You have to know your school and its students. In order to have made some of the best decisions, it was very important that I knew my school and its demographics. Again, study your school and know data. It is very important to know your kids and learn every single student and their names. They know me as Dr. Witt, so I set out to learn their names.

In the book *The Leadership Challenge,* Kouzes and Posner (2002) identify "Five Practices of Exemplary Leadership". Choose one of the five practices and explain how you currently demonstrate that practice.

Challenge the Process

My colleagues would all agree that I am a risk-taker. Why not challenge the process to continue to excel at greatness? I have always been challenged and taught to never be just comfortable. I am all about searching for opportunities, experimenting and taking risks to grow to the next level. True leaders venture out. I credit one principal I worked under for many years, Mr. Tilley. He always pushed me to think outside the box and/or to find a new approach to make things happen. Those who lead others to greatness seek and accept challenge. I am a leader who seeks innovative ways to change, grow and improve the organization. Change can be stressful but it is good. In doing so, we experiment and take risks. And because leaders know that risk taking involves mistakes and failures, they accept the inevitable disappointments as learning opportunities. Leaders are seeking innovation—new ways to improve the organization. I believe that my colleagues would enthusiastically say that I am always on the forefront of looking for ways to increase and improve student achievement.

What activities and learning experiences do you recommend for assistant principals aspiring to assume the role of principal?

As an administrator you must be visible, and be visible daily! Make it your point to see every teacher and every student every single day. Be present for morning drop-off, lunch, passing periods and dismissal. Visibility sets the tone of how you run the school and students know that you care. They also believe in their mind that Dr. Witt sees everything. Students and staff appreciate seeing you on a daily basis and confirm that you care about your school community and its stakeholders.

All decisions should be made in the best interest of students. Always focus on students first. While this seems to be an easy task, it is often where we forget that in the midst of doing what is easier for the adults. This is why it is key to have an advisory team that includes all stakeholders, including students.

Being transparent with all stakeholders brings a sense of ownership and respect. As aspiring principals, I recommend honoring confidentiality and not allowing division and distrust among your staff. Always do your best to put fires out before they spread across the school community.

Before we were administrators, we were teachers first. Get into those classrooms as often as you can. Teach a class as often as you can. Sometimes, I find value in going into classrooms and teaching for the period. It will help you stay grounded in what really matters and keeps your perspective on the kids. It also shows that we are team players and we really are there to help support and coach our teachers.

Last but not least, own your school. From clean bathrooms to high quality teachers to office friendly staff, own every piece of your school. Love it and create a school that you are proud to call your "own." Your best friends at your site will be your plant manager, campus security, and your officer manager. Just ask Charles, Ricky or Yisel, they truly were instrumental in my success during one of my past leadership roles. Make those relationships happen! Three important things to remember- do not micromanage, do not control and do not over delegate.

What do you believe are five (5) key characteristics of effective leadership? Describe how you demonstrate each of those characteristics.

We can go back and forth on what the key characteristics of effective leadership are all day. I really believe it depends on who you are, your experiences, what type of leadership theory you have embraced and your overall experience in your leadership roles. There are times where I feel that key characteristics vary. Today, I believe a leader should be **passionate, focused, empowering, communicative, and humble.**

It's possible to teach someone to be a leader, but to be truly effective you have to already be passionate about what you do. There were mentors that saw something in me, that helped me to realize that I had the passion to lead and pushed me to put that passion into motion. Thank you, Mr. Tilley, Ms. Carter, Ms. Kirk-Latham and Mr. Howard. Leaders with such passion gladly work countless hours, work against all odds and obstacles and successfully use their passion to achieve their overall objectives. Good leaders have a passion for the work they do and feel it is important. Sharing that passion and enthusiasm with my staff members has helped to motivate them to become more productive.

A focused leader leads their team to success. I find it to be important to eliminate distractions from the work area and to hone in on key issues that are affecting the school climate. We are often pulled in numerous directions simultaneously. But I always retain a clear meaning and focus on the things that matter. Being a focused leader helps me to plan ahead. I often find myself thinking through multiple scenarios and the impact of my decisions. This helps me to become prepared with established strategies, processes and routines so that high performance is easily definite.

You have to be a supportive leader and empower your team. My primary focus is to empower each individual by making it clear that I trust their judgment. I don't mind consulting and providing my answer, "In order for you to succeed I want to push you to do great." I strive to give people the authority they need to do their jobs well and show them an appropriate level of respect.

Leaders that communicate the direction and provide clear objectives build an overall picture that guides their schools towards greatness. I'm always transparent to the team on what's going on. Building your advisory and leadership teams allow for leaders to involve their staff in the important decisions that need to be made. You can't be the only voice at your school. You need feedback and input. Clear communication is the most important key to a leader's success. To grow as a leader, you must learn how to be an effective and compelling communicator.

My favorite, humility! Effective and respected school site administrators exhibit humbleness and compassion. You should also strive to understand where your staff are coming from and always keep a grounded perspective. When interacting with staff, I am always open to their opinions and needs. It's tough to be transparent and open- but in order to have great working relationships it's a must. Like many leadership skills, humility may not come easy to everyone. But self-reflection is key in order to succeed as a humble leader.

Lastly, I will say again micromanaging kills morale- and it's not very humble. Choose good people and train them. Get out of the way and let your staff do their job.

In the book *School Culture Rewired*, Steve Gruenert and Todd Whitaker (2015) explains the difference in school climate and school culture as the climate represents the weather today and school culture represents the weather over a long period of time.

When you walk on a school campus, you can immediately get a sense of the school climate and culture by watching the interactions between staff members and noticing the school's physical environment. The best start to acquiring a school and assessing the needs is to remain quiet and observe. Just as much as your assessing the culture and identifying needs, your stakeholders are watching to see how you are different from the last. It starts with trust, and is an essential prerequisite to a positive school culture. The first step is to put together an advisory team that will serve as your liaison to the school community. These members will provide historical and current insight as to where the school's climate and culture are. Creating a positive school climate is really hard to do. People have minds of their own, and you can't make them feel happy and optimistic on command.

Characteristics of a school with a positive climate and culture show people are engaged and respected. Students, families and educators work together to develop and live a shared school vision. Lastly, norms, values and expectations support social, emotional and physical safety.

What educational leaders are saying about Dr. Witt:

"Ms. Witt is a knowledgeable and dedicated professional with a proven commitment and talent for serving others within the field of education."

"I have had the opportunity to work with Ms. Witt both as colleague and as her supervisor for approximately ten years. During this time, I have known her to be a proactive and dedicated educator who has consistently put the needs of our students and staff above all else."

"Ms. Witt is resourceful, creative and a solution-oriented person. Her depth of knowledge and interaction with students demonstrated her leadership capacity. Her attention to detail, honesty and dedication should be applauded."

Born January 3, 1977 in Los Angeles, California La Shawn Denise Witt currently resides in Inglewood and works as an Assistant Principal in a local school district. She previously spent the last 16 years as a middle school life science teacher, assistant principal and teacher on special assignment in a neighboring district.

She currently holds two Bachelor degrees from Loyola Marymount University, two Master's degrees from Mount Saint Mary's College and Pepperdine University, and a Doctorate in Educational Leadership from Argosy University.

She is the single mother to one child, Morgan who is a sophomore at Howard University in Washington, D.C. Morgan is studying African American Studies and History with aspirations to become a Civil Rights Attorney. Morgan is also the official school disc jockey at Howard.

She is an active and proud member of Delta Sigma Theta Sorority-Inglewood Alumnae Chapter, Jack and Jill of America where she serves as the Inglewood Associate Chapter's Correspondence Secretary and Event Coordinator, Tabahani Book Circle, Phi Delta Kappa Sorority, Inc., National Association of University Women and The Links, Incorporated. She currently attends West Angeles Church of God In Christ.

Outside of her professional and personal commitments, La Shawn indulges in her passions of shopping, traveling, reading, doing community service and enjoying time with the loves of her life, daughter Morgan, and Shih Tzu's Dolce and Gabbana. She is very active with her sorority and has aspirations of National Leadership.

In addition, she owns a wedding and special event business based out of Beverly Hills, California, with satellite locations throughout the country. It was her dream to provide clients around the country with quality event planning that they could trust at an affordable rate. After working in the event industry for the past 22 years, she has established a reputation of being dependable and trustworthy, has produced over 450 events, and maintains working relationships with many of Los Angeles's top event industry professionals. La Shawn is an event scholar that makes sure all of her events shine and the guests go home wanting more. La Shawn sees each event as a unique opportunity to design the experience of a lifetime and give clients a personalized and elegant event.

She describes herself as being ambitious, personable, and easy to work with. She is also punctual and very hard working, self-motivated and driven to follow tasks through to completion.

"If your actions inspire others to dream more, learn more, do more and become more, you are a leader." – John Quincy Adams

Conclusion

There it is! In the voice of nine assistant principals that aspire to take the helm and become Next In Line to Lead! These assistant principals are working diligently and with great intention to learn all they can about the principalship while serving as assistant principals.

In addition to their duties and responsibilities as assistant principals, these assistant principal are dedicated to their families and involved with their communities. Most have found time to not only excel as an educator, but to also use their talents and skills to start their own business, foundation, or program.

I applaud school districts across the country who are making a deliberate effort to not only develop assistant principals as leaders but also, prepare them to assume the role of principal.

Preparing to Lead: My Advice to Aspiring Principals

As mentioned in the Preface, preparing assistant principals for the principalship is an educational passion. Assistant principals bring various levels and background experience from their role as a classroom teacher or teacher leader. The role of assistant principal is the most common pathway to the principalship. I wholeheartedly believe that school districts should have an intentional and deliberate focus on preparing assistant principals to lead schools. Leadership development is paramount. Leadership involves influence.

"Without influence, leadership does not exist!" – Peter G. Northouse

My advice to Aspiring Principals is to **L.E.A.D.**

Learn. Learn. Continue to Learn.

"Leadership and learning are indispensable to each other" – John, F. Kennedy

Aspiring principals must learn all they can about the principalship and effective leadership. You must learn to establish a vision and be able to effectively communicate that vision. Aspiring leaders must learn to take risks and create an environment where staff will also feel comfortable to take risks.

Aspiring leaders must learn from experiences (your own and others). You must learn humility. When you practice humility, you recognize your areas of growth and rely on the expertise of others to complement. The focus should be on developing your strengths, but you must be aware of your limitations. You need to continue to learn best practices in leadership. You must learn to find your leadership voice. You must be a lifelong learner!

Empower. Engage. Equip.

"A leader is great, not because of his or her power, but because of his or her ability to empower others" – John Maxwell

You are empowered when you are confident in your own ability and knowledge (Cunningham & Gresso, 1993). Leaders are most effective when they empower others to lead. You must allow your staff to take ownership in their own decisions and choices.

Leadership is found in your daily actions. Engagement is making connections. You must connect with students, staff, district leaders, parents and the community. Are you visible and accessible; or are you behind closed doors of your office? Do you attend community events? This is especially important if you are a leader in a small community. Do you know who the town, county, or city officials are? Do they know who you are?

Are you "Equipped to Serve?" According to Ken Blanchard (2006), ego keeps you from becoming a servant leader. The ego is undoubtedly, the biggest barrier to leadership. You cannot lead effectively while self-promoting. You must continually develop others and focus on the improvement of the school. Relationships with all stakeholders are important and your leadership is based on trust. You can choose to be self-serving or you can choose to serve.

Authenticity. Accountability. Assessment

"Accountability Breeds Response-Ability" – Stephen R. Covey

No one can do this job alone. No one... authentic leadership improves quality and effectiveness. It encourages and builds honest relationships. It eliminates working in silos. When you have true relationships as a leader, information is shared more freely, you will find there is intentional communication amongst the staff and it encourages teamwork.

Accountability is simply taking responsibility for your actions and decisions. You must identify and acknowledge your strengths, limitations, beliefs, and core values. Accountability will enable you to reflect and identify any necessary adjustments based on evidence. When you are accountable, you set goals and communicate then consistently.

Assessing where you are as a leader allows you to make the necessary improvements. Are you aware of your leadership style? Have you assessed and reflected on your capabilities as a leader? What are your opportunities for growth? Are you able to effectively communicate with all stakeholders? Are you able to appropriately collect, analyze, and interpret data? Are you a problem-solver, a strategic thinker? Are you able to resolve conflict? I am an advocate of self-assessment and reflection. Improvements are made through reflection and assessment

Development. Data-Driven. Diligence

"Few things are impossible to diligence and skill. Great works are performed not by strength, but by perseverance." – Samuel Johnson

Aspiring principals must develop in several key areas while serving as assistant principals. Developing your role as an instructional leader is imperative. The days are gone when assistant principals only focused on tasks such as discipline, buses, and substitutes. The role of the assistant principal has definitely evolved. I was an assistant principal in the early 2000s. I can recall the shift at that time. Increased accountability, instructional responsibilities, as well as federal and state mandates are all factors that have contributed to the shift in roles for school leaders.

Data must guide and inform decisions in all areas of education. Using data effectively and appropriately can lead to improved student performance. Effective data use must be modeled in addition to providing learning opportunities to teachers in the effective use of data.

Diligence is required in leadership. Discipline promotes diligence. You start with a vision, create a plan, and then you execute the plan. Without diligence, there can be no true leadership.

It is important to note that assistant principals do not often times have formal authority of their own responsibilities. Assistant principals are not "in charge" of schools. They do; however, in most cases, have responsibility of various grade levels, content areas, or departments. You must remember, you are an assistant PRINCIPAL and NOT a principal's ASSISTANT. I charge you to find your leadership voice and identify yourself as a leader. You cannot wait until you are appointed principal to begin developing these skills.

Communicate your career goals to your principal. If you are not gaining the necessary experience in your school building to enhance and develop critical leadership skills, you should take it upon yourself to identify a mentor and/or coach or will assist you in that development if you have not been assigned one in your school district. I also urge you to gain experience in more than one program area or grade level structure.

As an effective leader, you must set boundaries and maintain an appropriate work-life balance. Time-management is one of the most challenging areas that I hear from new principals and regarding the need to improve. The calendar is your friend. You have to use it and do not deviate it from it. Schedule everything. Yes, everything. Identify and prioritize your goals daily, weekly, monthly, quarterly, and yearly. You must determine the tasks that are both important and urgent. When you identify those tasks, it will become clear as to what you can delegate. I often refer to Covey's Time-Management Matrix. The matrix allows you to organize your priorities into four categories: Urgent & Important, Not Urgent & Important, Urgent & Not Important, Not Urgent & Not Important.

The quickest way to burnout is not having a healthy work-life balance. You will begin to feel like you are not accomplishing tasks. When you are trying to do too much at once, you will feel overwhelmed. Focus on one task at a time. Research has indicated that multitasking can negatively affect leadership

In many ways. The key to productivity is in your ability to focus on what's most important at the moment. I am defining multitasking as attempting to do two or more things simultaneously that requires your focused attention.

You have to address culture when implementing change. Culture is critical to the success of change management. Leaders shape culture by everything that is done, said, allowed and everything that is not done, said, and allowed. In order to change the school's culture you must understand the existing culture.

Finally, no matter what experience you have and how much someone is mentoring or coaching you, the reality of the duties and responsibilities of a principal will not be realized until you are sitting in the seat. I do not think you will ever be totally prepared to assume the role of principal, but there should be some level of readiness for the principalship that you experience as an assistant principal.

During the process of completing this book, Damon Qualls was appointed principal of an elementary school in his current school district for the 2017-2018 School Year. Damon, I congratulate you and wish you nothing but continued blessings and success as you begin your principalship. Just remember two things: 1. Expectations are best met when they are communicated and clear. 2. Relationships are the key ingredient to successful leadership. Principal Damon Qualls...This is YOUR time!

As I conclude this book, I invite you to be a part of the *Next In Line to Lead* book series. Upcoming volumes will include: *The Voice of the Newly-Appointed Principal*, *The Voice of the Supervising Principal*, *The Voice of the Leadership Development Coach*, and *The Voice of the Superintendent*.

If you are an assistant principal that aspire to assume the role of principal, you are also invited to be a part of the Second Edition of *Next In Line to Lead: The Voice of the Assistant Principal*.

You may visit www.nextinlinetolead.com or contact us at info@nextinlinetolead.com for additional information.

"Before you are a leader, success is all about growing yourself. When you become a leader, success is all about growing others." – Jack Welch

ABOUT THE CREATOR OF NEXT IN LINE TO LEAD

Dr. Sharon Hargro Porter

"Leaders are most effective when they empower others to lead." – S. Porter

Dr. Sharon Hargro Porter resides in the Washington, D.C. metropolitan area. She has served as an educator for over 25 years. She currently serves as a Leadership Development Coach for novice principals and assistant principals and coordinates an induction program for first and second year assistant principals in a large urban school district. She is a former elementary and middle school principal.

Sharon is the CEO and Owner of **Perfect Time SHP LLC, Coaching and Consulting Firm**, Founder of the **Global Relationships Igniting Networks and Development (GRIND) Entrepreneur Network**, and Creator and Host of the **Write the Book Now! Interview and Podcast Show.**

Sharon earned a Bachelor of Science (B.S.) in Elementary Education at Winston-Salem State University, a Master of Education (M.Ed.) in Curriculum & Instruction at National-Louis University, Administration & Supervision Post Graduate Certification at the Johns Hopkins University, an Educational Specialist (Ed.S.) degree at Walden University, and a Doctorate of Education (Ed.D.) in Educational Leadership & Policy Studies from Howard University. Her dissertation title is: *Preparing the Next In Line: New Principals' Perceptions of a School District's District-Run Principal Preparation Programs.*

Sharon is a National Association of Elementary School Principal (NAESP) Certified Principal Mentor and is a Gallup-Certified Strengths Coach. She holds a School Superintendent Endorsement from the State of Maryland and holds current educational licenses in Maryland and North Carolina.

Sharon is married to her husband Larry, a bonus-mom to Sydney, and a pet mom to her adorable Bichon, CoCo Cotton.

She is a proud member of Delta Sigma Theta Sorority, Incorporated.

Supporters for **Next In Line to Lead (Vol. 1)**

SANDRA BOBO

Howard Gasaway III

Jamia Bobo

Jayla Bobo

Katrina Lamont

Wayne Lassiter

Monique Jeffery

Kristi Holden, Ed.D.

Carletta Marrow, Ed.D.

Ed Ryans. Ed.D.

Sharron Credle, Ed.D.

Daria Valentine, Ed.D.

Sharon H. Porter, Ed.D.

Jereneze Campbell, Ed.D.

Rudolph Saunders, Ed.D.

Kirsten Anderson Simpkins

Ramona Burton

Tara Giles Callands

Rhonda Johnson

Julian A. Jackson

Elaine Rhem

Dionne Doby

Reshan Powell

Aaron Cardwell

DARREN CLAY

Albert and Valerie Nelson

Anthony Newbold

Brianna Clay

Candice Clay

Carolyn Greer

Carlene Millen

Donald Fennoy, III

Earnest and Shirley Gordon

Eric Hollinhead

Gary M. Clay, Sr.

Gary M. Clay, Jr.

James and Deborah Carter

Jamil Jean-Louis

LECINDA JENNINGS

Sharon Johnson

Sadie Richardson

Marlena Gore

Kim LaTrell Ryans, M.Ed, NCC — kryans@acpsd.net

Tamara Jones — Instagram: luckyducks2650

Lucky Ducks — Fb page: luckyducks

Malachi J. Conyers

Henrietta Green

Genine Blue

Ericka Ashley Bennett

DAMON QUALLS

George Champlin, — Twitter: @G_Champlin
Principal Slater Marietta Elementary

Hanna Sweatt, M.Ed, Ed.S. — Twitter:@hannalee2163
Greenville County Schools

Jenna Key — Twitter:@jennalkey
Greenville County School District

Dr. Michael Fleming
Retired Principal and Adjunct Professor

Wakesha Fogle — Twitter:@wakeshafogle

WAKE Academy and Consulting LLC

Mr. and Mrs. Willie & Loretta Qualls

Natalie Qualls-Johnson

Kristy L. Qualls, Principal   Twitter:@KristyLQualls
Pelham Road Elementary School

DR. NAJLA SOLOMON

MeL McKenzie
Rebel President / Cofounder of Warriors On 2s MC

Patricia King-Gibbs, MSW

Michael Solomon

Simone Goode

Kelisha Brooks

Delethia Lloyd,
NP – Adult- Gerontology Nurse Practitioner

Olivia Tsampis

George Castlewood

DeAndre Jones

Erika Rokes

Shanique Walls

Michele Jones

Tamika Jordan

Aatifa Castro

Thomas Gourdine

Idrissa Castlewood

Antisha Nesbit

Yasmeen Ash

Fay Carr

Justina Hay-Parlay Living

April Lewis

Dorothy Conners

Rashawn Adams

Roxanne Medina

Shareefah Rokes

Shareida Tarver

Malaika Thompson

Devon Reed

Felicia Moody

Erika Francis
Darcell Castlewood
Quamirah Castro
Shonday Rokes

NATASHA MCDONALD

Chester Herod
Ella Herod
Richard McDonald
Amari and Addisyn Simmons
Sheri Herod
Donald Battee
Georgie Herod
Erica Brown
Vincent Dias
Ella "Tootie" Brown
John Gay
Jadel Jones
Arkeil Jones
Kaliel Thomas
Ashanti Holland
Cairobian Gay
Jacyrus Gay
Dion Williams
Chantel Terrell
Richard and Joyce McDonald
John and Shayla McDonald
Emmanuel and Mavis Thomas
Vincent Herod
Todd and Beverly Mohair
Brandon and Stephanie Mohair
Jay and Naborina Flowers
Detrich and Maiya Moseley
Kedric and Maryanne Battee'
Joel and LaTonya Cruz
Shaunna McHenry
Norbert and Baneca Nyereyemhuka

Markeba Warfield
Janaye Easter
Bryant and Candi Mattherson
Tiffany Massey
Marcia Bell
Alvin and Nita Cates
Cen10 Admin
(Alicia Maphies, David Alexander, Clint Cypert, Matt Sears and Tony Farmer)
Avery Jones
Shirley Davis
Leon Roddy
Philip and Tina Moore
Courtney and Danielle Record
Michael and Julie Duncan
Joel Robertson
Cody and Maura Ayres
Chrys and Letycia Fowler
Todd and Jasma Hayes
Ronald Brown
Billie Mohair

DR. LA SHAWN D. WITT
Elder Willie Witt
Sharon Witt
Kevin Witt
Morgan Williams
Brent Tilley
Inglewood Unified School District
Sherryl Carter
Inglewood Unified School District
LaTanya Kirk Latham
Beverly Hills Unified School District
Ricky Wright
Gaylin Munford
Inglewood Unified School District
Dr. Diane Watkins

DR. SHARON HARGRO PORTER

Perfect Time SHP, LLC — Twitter @PerfectTimeSHP

The GRIND Entrepreneur Network — Twitter @GrindeNetwork

Write the Book Now!
Write the Book Now! Interview and Podcast Show — Twitter: @writethebooknow

James Adell
James Adell Photography — Twitter @jamesadellphoto

Deshardior Studio Spa

Michelle Boyd Hauser

Joann H. Hargro

Wendy Buckley

Jerald L. Hoover
Jerald L. Hoover Productions, LLC — Twitter: @JeraldHooverSports

Nikkie W. Miller — Twitter@nikkimiller1913
Assistant Principal-Pitt County Schools-Greenville, NC

Made in the USA
Columbia, SC
09 July 2017